Steps to
Successful
Reading:
Nonfiction

Margaret Cleveland

J. WESTON
WALCH
PUBLISHER

Portland, Maine

Acknowledgments

Thanks go to the editorial staff at J. Weston Walch, Publisher, particularly Holly Moirs, Ann Shea, and Susan Blair. Also, my heartfelt appreciation to Mary Rich, who did a masterful copyediting job. My special thanks to Lisa French, Alan Lyscars, and Kate O'Halloran for their support and help on the project.

This book is dedicated to Alex and Jake, my very favorite readers.

User's Guide
to
Walch Reproducible Books

As part of our general effort to provide educational materials that are as practical and economical as possible, we have designated this publication a "reproducible book." The designation means that purchase of the book includes purchase of the right to limited reproduction of all pages on which this symbol appears:

Here is the basic Walch policy: We grant to individual purchasers of this book the right to make sufficient copies of reproducible pages for use by all students of a single teacher. This permission is limited to a single teacher and does not apply to entire schools or school systems, so institutions purchasing the book should pass the permission on to a single teacher. Copying of the book or its parts for resale is prohibited.

Any questions regarding this policy or requests to purchase further reproduction rights should be addressed to:

Permissions Editor
J. Weston Walch, Publisher
321 Valley Street • P. O. Box 658
Portland, Maine 04104-0658

CONTENTS

TO THE TEACHER

Welcome to *Steps to Successful Reading: Nonfiction.*

Your students are bombarded with written messages all day long. In the classroom, they are called upon to read in every subject area—and to comprehend and retain what they've read. Beyond the classroom, they are asked to read directions, newspapers, articles, applications, stories, letters, e-mails, and research from the Internet, from their friends, from businesses, and from their community.

Reading and the language arts are the most important tools your students have in their repertoire as they extend their life in the classroom and beyond. Without the tools to become a discerning reader, your students will not experience the world around them as fully as they can. Becoming a good reader means experiencing life more fully.

Steps to Successful Reading: Nonfiction and *Fiction* were written to help students gain control of their reading so that they feel confident as readers. These books were written to pique your students' interest; they were written to invite your students to interact and to engage with their reading and with various genres, words, strategies, skills, critical thinking, and assessments.

How Students Become Better Readers

Research shows that fluent readers have several things in common:

1. They read with a purpose to get information, to be entertained, to learn steps in a process.
2. They read quickly and fluently, automatically recognizing letters and words without having to stop and decode them.
3. They use a variety of strategies to read efficiently, depending on the type of text and purpose of their reading.
4. They use their own prior knowledge to engage with the text and derive meaning from it.
5. They use various critical-thinking strategies, such as analysis and evaluation, synthesis and application, to interact with the text and determine their own agreement or disagreement with the author.

Steps to Successful Reading: Nonfiction and its companion *Steps to Successful Reading: Fiction* offer a number of strategies, skills, and practice to help your reluctant readers feel more confident in their reading, with the goal of increasing fluency. Reflecting the English/Language Arts Standards, the lessons follow a natural sequence, building skill upon skill so that each chapter will naturally call for practice of the newly acquired or reinforced skill from the prior lesson. In the matrix on page *viii,* you will find a breakdown of what skills are taught in each lesson. You will also find a correlation of critical-thinking skills that are emphasized in each lesson. The questions and the reading skills taught encourage students to use these critical-thinking processes.

Standards-Based Instruction

The six lessons in *Steps to Successful Reading: Nonfiction* correlate and reflect the current national English/Language Arts Standards. All of the language arts standards are touched on in some way throughout the book. Below is a list of the standards that lend themselves particularly to *Steps,* and an annotation of how the lessons correlate to each national standard:

Standard 1

Students read a wide range of print and nonprint texts to build an understanding of texts, of themselves, and of the cultures of the United States and the world; to acquire new information; to respond to the needs and demands of society and the workplace; and for personal fulfillment. Among these texts are fiction and nonfiction, classic and contemporary works.

The lessons in *Steps to Successful Reading: Nonfiction* offer a variety of nonfiction readings including **biography, interview, on-line encyclopedia, newspaper column, speech,** and **advertisement.** These specific sub-genres of nonfiction were chosen specifically because they are engaging and interesting and because they represent a wide spectrum of nonfiction materials representative of what students will encounter in the real world.

Standard 3

Students apply a wide range of strategies to comprehend, interpret, evaluate, and appreciate texts. They draw on their prior experience, their interactions with other readers and writers, their knowledge of word meaning and of other texts, their word identification strategies, and their understanding of textual features.

This standard is reflected throughout the pages of this book. In every lesson, students are given a new strategy, a new skill, and mechanisms for assessing their understanding in many ways, using a variety of intelligences.

Step 1 is called **Link It.** This is a prereading strategy where students find a way to link what they already know to what they are about to learn. Questions, discussion, analysis, and engagement with the subject bring students to the new excerpt, preparing them for their new reading. Several

lessons instruct and reinforce word clues, context clues, and vocabulary, making decoding easier. This text presumes that students are literate and are reading at an approximate 3–6 grade level. The lessons are scaffolded, building on one another, but it is important to note that each lesson can be taught independently or in sequence, depending on your or your students' needs or desires.

Standard 5

Students employ a wide range of strategies as they write and use different writing process elements appropriately to communicate with different audiences for a variety of purposes.

In each of the lessons in *Steps,* one of the **Relate It** activities is a writing extension. Here students have an opportunity to reflect on, to imitate, and to extend their reading and understanding into their own written work. They will brainstorm, draft, and publish various types of writing for various purposes and audiences to extend their reading comprehension and writing skills. An important part of writing is reading, and we didn't leave this out!

Standard 6

Students apply knowledge of language structure, language conventions, media techniques, figurative language, and genre to create, critique, and discuss print and nonprint texts.

Steps first offers a variety of genres as well as types of language and uses of language. In several lessons—Speech and Columns in particular—students analyze the use of literary devices and language to understand how these elements enhance the writing and the reading experience.

Standard 7

Students conduct research on issues and interests by generating ideas and questions, and by posing problems. They gather, evaluate, and synthesize data from a variety of sources to communicate their discoveries in ways that suit their purpose and audience.

Steps reflects this standard in various ways. **Step 5: Relate It** offers students a way to extend their understanding of the lesson content, skill, and strategy beyond the classroom through technology and/or research using their speaking or listening skills and applying one of the multiple intelligences. **Step 3: Assess It** offers students a chance to not only comprehend and recall what they have read, but to apply test-taking strategies by generating their own tests in various styles, including multiple choice, short answer, true/false, essay, and analogy formats. Given the opportunity to create these assessments for their classmates, students will make these strategies their own so that when they encounter them on a variety of state or national standardized tests, they will be familiar with the format and the intent of the tests.

Standard 8

Students use a variety of technological and information resources to gather and synthesize information and to create and communicate knowledge.

Each **Step 5: Relate It** offers students various ways to use the Internet or other research tools to extend their knowledge of the content or context (skills) of their reading. At the end of the **Relate It** extensions, you will see icons that are quick references to the various learning styles.

Standard 10

Students whose first language is not English make use of their first language to develop competency in English language arts and to develop understanding of content across the curriculum.

In each lesson's Teacher Guide, you will find a section called **Especially for English Language Learners.** *Steps* goes beyond the standard here to invite non-native speakers to discuss cultural and language issues with their classmates. Using these suggestions will help you to unite your native and non-native speakers.

Standard 11

Students participate as knowledgeable, reflective, creative, and critical members of a variety of literacy communities.

Your students will be embarking on a great journey of reading nonfiction as they experience this book. After each reading, they are invited to react to their reading, accessing their personal response and making the material their own. Throughout, students are asked what they think, how they respond, what the reading means to them. Good reading will only come when students feel that they are a part of what they read. The stories or the articles they read must have meaning for them or they will never engage. It is our hope that *Steps to Successful Reading* will give your students the essential skills, tools, strategies, and variety to engage with, be inspired, and feel confident about their reading.

MATRIX OF STRATEGIES/SKILLS/ TESTS/CRITICAL-THINKING SKILLS

	Lesson 1: Biography	Lesson 2: Interview	Lesson 3: On-line Research Article	Lesson 4: Newspaper Columns	Lesson 5: Speech	Lesson 6: Advertisements
LEARNING STRATEGY						
Skimming/Making Predictions	●	●	●	●	●	●
Setting a Purpose	●	●	●	●	●	●
Gathering Evidence		●	●	●	●	●
Recognizing Word Clues			●	●	●	●
Using Context Clues			●	●	●	●
Summarizing				●	●	●
Recognizing Setting					●	
Finding Point of View						
Reading Between the Lines						●
READING SKILLS						
Identifying Main Idea/Details	●	●	●	●	●	●
Drawing Conclusions		●	●	●	●	●
Making Inferences			●	●	●	●
Making Generalizations			●	●	●	●
Comparing and Contrasting				●	●	●
Understanding Use of Literary Devices					●	
Discovering Tone					●	
Recognizing Fact/Nonfact/Claim						●
TEST-TAKING STRATEGY						
True/False	●					
Short Answer Synthesis		●				
Multiple Choice			●			
Personal Response Essay				●		
Recall/Comprehension					●	
Short Answer Evaluation						●
CRITICAL-THINKING SKILLS						
Recall	●	●	●		●	●
Comprehension	●	●	●		●	●
Application			●	●	●	●
Analysis		●	●	●	●	●
Synthesis		●		●	●	●
Evaluation				●	●	●

BIOGRAPHY

"MAYA LIN: SCULPTOR"
(from *16 Extraordinary Asian Americans* by Nancy Lobb)

Learning Strategy:	Predicting/Setting a Purpose for Reading
Reading Skill:	Identifying the Main Idea and Supporting Details
Test-Taking Strategy:	True/False

Setting the Scene

Maya Lin was just 21 when she won a competition to design the Vietnam Veterans Memorial in Washington, D.C. She received her degree in architecture and went on to design several other important national monuments. Maya Lin is one among many artists who have contributed to the psyche of the American landscape through her artwork.

As you introduce the lesson, engage students in a discussion about art and monuments in their community. You may want to have them name several of these monuments and review some factual information about them. If there is time, you may want to visit a monument as a class field trip. Ask students to discuss the importance that public art has in their own lives and in the lives of the community.

Many students may never have really noticed the artwork in their area before; they may see it as part of the landscape without really paying attention to it. Encourage your learners to become more aware of the human-made landscape around them. Have them take a good look *up* at the buildings in their town or city. Often there are architectural elements that go unnoticed at street level. Invite the class to think about what their community—or any community—would be like without the work of sculptors, architects, or artists to help create a feeling, a landscape, or a particular "look" in their community.

Introducing the Skill

The most important skill necessary for reading nonfiction is introduced in this first lesson: understanding the main idea and supporting details. Once students have mastered this skill, they will be able to move forward and analyze and evaluate their reading. Be sure that your learners have a full grasp of this concept. Graphic organizers are a great way to illustrate the connection between main idea and supporting details. Encourage your learners to think of ways to illustrate main idea and details through graphic organizers—such as a web, or even a table (with the top as the main idea and the legs as supporting details). Invite students to be creative.

One way to illustrate the relevance of the main idea and details in your students' reading is to work with magazine articles, newspapers, or reading from their other subject areas. Have them read aloud to the class from a selection of their choosing and ask the class to state the main idea. Or, you could bring in a copy of a newspaper and ask students to skim through headlines to see what the main ideas are in the news. Another way to introduce the skill is to show learners a photograph and ask them to determine the main idea of the photograph. You could invite them to give the photo a title to reflect its main idea. NOTE: Be sure to begin all of your discussions on reading with a check-in to be sure that your learners understand the main idea. This skill will be reinforced throughout the lessons in this book.

Especially for English Language Learners

Sharing Culture Invite your English Language Learners to describe a monument or sculpture that they remember from their country of origin. What did that monument commemorate? Ask them to share further about how the arts were reflected in their society. Were artists revered? Were they well paid? Or were they considered part of the "fringes" of society? Establish common ground with your English Language Learners and your native speakers as they explore the messages that are conveyed by the monuments in their communities or former communities. Point out the similarities between cultures in terms of *why* people erect statues or monuments (for example, to celebrate fallen war heroes or powerful political leaders).

Sharing Language It is important that you preview particular words for English Language Learners so that they are able to discern the main idea of the article on Maya Lin. Some words to preview are listed in the next column. Ask your ELLs first to define any of these words that they know. Then ask your native speakers to help describe what the words mean. You

might also ask your ELLs to share what these words are in their first language.

controversial	civil rights
architecture	spiral
competition	fiber-optic
anonymous	

Assessing Understanding

True/False questions are designed to help students recall important facts about what they have read. This type of question does not require a high level of critical thinking; however, true/false questions do require a basic understanding of the main idea and important supporting details.

Chances are that most of your students will have had some exposure to true/false questions in the past. Remind them that they must go to the text to find the answers—that the answer is directly related to what they read, not necessarily to what *they think* the answer should be.

Reading Further

"An Emotive Place Apart," by Robert Campbell, *A.I.A. Journal*, May 1983.
The Photography of Architecture, Twelve Views, by Akido Busch, New York: Van Nostrand Reinhold.
Maya Lin: Architect and Artist, by Mary Malone, Springfield, NJ: Enslow Publishers.

Extending to Technology

To find more information about Maya Lin, conduct on-line searches using the following terms: Maya Lin, national monuments, and Washington, D.C. monuments. Or visit the following web sites:
www.who2.com/mayalin
www.womensire.com/watch/lin
www.nps.gov/vive/hom

BIOGRAPHY

"MAYA LIN: SCULPTOR"
(from *16 Extraordinary Asian Americans* by Nancy Lobb)

Learning Strategy:	Predicting/Setting a Purpose for Reading
Reading Skill:	Identifying the Main Idea and Supporting Details
Test-Taking Strategy:	True/False

STEP 1: LINK IT

Before You Read

Where are you sitting right now? Are you at home, at school, in a library, on a bus? If you are in a library or a school building, perhaps there is a statue or a sculpture somewhere inside or in front of the building. If you are at home or on the road, is there a statue or a sculpture you will pass by today? Or perhaps in the building where you are, there's a piece of artwork hanging in the front hallway. Somewhere near you, chances are, there is at least one piece of art.

People have been decorating buildings, erecting monuments, and creating statues as long as there have been dwellings. Even buildings themselves are pieces of art. Artists create these pieces of public art to allow the community to celebrate or commemorate people or events. Sometimes community art is a way to enhance the building where it is housed. What statues, monuments, or other works of art are in your community? What messages do they offer about your neighborhood, town, city, or buildings? How do they enhance the community's experience of the buildings or parks where they are?

You are about to read about Maya Lin, a young sculptor and architect, who at age 21 became famous when she won a competition to design the Vietnam Veterans Memorial in Washington, D.C. As you read, look for clues about why Lin might have created her monument the way she did. What message do you think her monument offers those who visit it?

Set a Strategy

Look over the excerpt on pages 6–8. Don't read it yet—just look it over quickly, reading only the first few words of each paragraph. This quick read is called **skimming.** You are only skimming the surface of the selection, not reading in depth. Now, make a prediction—a guess—about what you think the article is about. Write down four things that your skimming suggests to you. Don't worry about whether you are right or not. You'll have a chance to check your predictions later.

1. <u>Outrage upon hearing she was Chinese -American</u>
2. <u>Monument went from being hated to loved</u>
3. <u>Use of water in works</u>
4. _____

Set a Purpose

People write for three reasons: **to entertain, to persuade,** or **to inform.** People read for many reasons. They read a novel or story to be entertained. They read advertising to decide whether to buy something. They read books with facts in them to be informed. They read cookbooks to learn how to make a dish. They read poetry or essays to be inspired. People often have more than one purpose for reading. Sometimes they will read for information and entertainment. They may read to learn something and for inspiration.

Before you read anything, ask yourself two questions. The first is, **What kind of writing is this?** Is it a story, a novel, a newspaper article, an advertisement, a personal essay? This question will help you determine why the author wrote the selection. For example, if you are reading a story, you know you are reading for entertainment and not for information. If you are reading a cookbook, you may be reading for inspiration, entertainment, and/or to get specific information on how to cook a dish.

The second question you need to ask is, **Why am I reading this?** This question will help you become aware of your own purpose for reading. Are you reading for fun? Are you reading for information? Are you reading to learn something?

The reason it is important to find out why you are reading a selection is to decide how closely to read the selection. If you are reading a factual account, you may want to read more closely than if you were reading a cartoon. What is meant by *reading closely?* It means that you pay attention to the details or try to understand all of the article.

The selection you are about to read is a **biography.** Biographies are factual accounts of events in a person's life. This biography of Maya Lin focuses on one aspect of her life—her art—and specifically the creation of the Vietnam Veterans Memorial. Let's start with asking the important questions.

- **What kind of writing is this?** *You already know the selection is a biography, so it is a factual account. You know you will have to read the selection fairly closely.*

- **Why am I reading this?** POSSIBLE ANSWERS: *Because it is an assigned reading . . . Because I have seen the Vietnam Veterans Memorial and am interested in learning how it was created . . . Because I love to learn something new . . . Because I don't know anything about the Vietnam War and would like to know something about it . . . Because I saw the monument and didn't understand why people thought it was so great . . . Because I like to sculpt and want to find out how Maya Lin made it big . . .*

Now fill in some answers of your own:

I want to learn about Maya Lin because

interested

_____

_____

_____

STEP 2: READ IT

The following is an excerpt from 16 Extraordinary Asian Americans *by Nancy Lobb.*

The creative process isn't about sitting at a desk and waiting for an idea to hit you. Sometimes an idea will come to you after eight months of stewing over it—it's suddenly there. Artwork is very much research, reading, and then letting it sift through your head.

—Maya Lin

When she was still a student, Maya Lin became one of the most controversial artists in the world. At first, many people did not like her design for the Vietnam Veterans Memorial in Washington, D.C. Now, it has become a beloved national shrine. More people visit this monument each year than any other in the entire
5   country.

Lin was born in 1959 in Athens, Ohio. Her parents had come to America in the 1940s from China. Both taught at Ohio University. Her father was a ceramist and dean of the art school. Her mother was a poet and literature professor.

As a child, Maya enjoyed hiking, bird-watching, and reading. She also worked
10   in her father's pottery studio. In high school, she worked at a [fast-food] restaurant after school.

She was a gifted student. She especially loved math and art. After high school, she went to Yale University.

At Yale, Maya Lin wanted to major in both sculpture and architecture. The
15   school would not allow her to do this. So she enrolled in the architecture program. But she kept on taking sculpture classes.

In 1980, a nationwide contest was held to design the Vietnam Veterans Memorial. One of Lin's professors asked the students in his class to enter designs.

The memorial was to be built in Washington, D.C. The site was between the
20   Lincoln Memorial and the Capitol.

Lin went to Washington to study the building site. The beautiful, grassy area gave her a peaceful, calm feeling. She knew she wanted to keep that feeling in her work.

Her final design was two long, black granite walls. The walls came together to
25 form a giant V. On the wall were the names of the 58,000 men and women who
were killed or missing in action in the war. The names were written in the order
in which they died or were reported missing.

Over 1,400 artists entered the competition. The names of the artists were not
revealed to the judges.

30 On May 6, 1981, the winning entry was announced. It was Lin. At the time, she
was a senior at Yale. And she was totally unknown in the art world.

Some Vietnam veterans were unhappy with the choice. They wanted a more
traditional statue—perhaps something with soldiers on it. Her design was called
a "wall of shame."

35 But it got worse. When the protesters found out that Lin was a Chinese-
American woman, they were outraged. Many sexist and racist slurs were directed
at her.

Lin was shocked and hurt. She had always thought of herself as just another
American college student. She had never felt the sting of racial prejudice before.

40 In her own words:

"The competition was anonymous. No names were allowed on any of the
boards. It has always been a question in my mind as to what would've happened
if names had been allowed. I hope sometime that people's names can be left on
and it won't make a difference . . ." (as quoted in *The Chinese Americans*).

45 The debate went on for nearly a year. Finally, a compromise was reached. The
wall would be built as Lin had designed it. But a more traditional monument
would be added near the entrance to the memorial site.

The Vietnam Veterans Memorial was dedicated November 13, 1982. Lin's name
was not even mentioned during the ceremony.

50 But all that changed as people began visiting the memorial. Thousands came to
find the names of their loved ones killed in the war. Many made rubbings of the
engraved names. The memorial became a place of healing.

In 1987, Lin was asked to design a memorial in Montgomery, Alabama, for
those who had died in the civil rights struggle. She began studying the civil
55 rights movement. She read the works of Dr. Martin Luther King, Jr.

In 1963, Dr. King gave his famous "I have a dream" speech. In that speech,
King said, "We will not be satisfied . . . until justice rolls down like waters and

righteousness like a mighty stream." Lin was inspired by the image of rolling water.

60   She designed the monument in two parts. First there was a black granite disk about 12 feet across. On it were written 21 important events in the civil rights movement. Forty people who died in the struggle were listed.

    Behind the disk was the second part of the monument. It was a nine-foot wall with King's quotation engraved on it. Both pieces were covered with a thin sheet

65 of very slowly moving water.

    The Civil Rights Memorial was dedicated in 1989. Lin was surprised and moved when people began to cry during the ceremony. Again she had created a place where healing could take place.

    Her fame was spreading. During the 1990s Lin completed a number of different

70 projects.

    Yale University asked her to design a sculpture to honor women at the school. Lin's design was a three-foot-high table of green granite. Water seeped through a hole in the center of the table.

    On top of the table was a spiral of numbers. The numbers showed how many

75 women were enrolled at Yale for each year since the college was founded in 1701.

    But no women were allowed into Yale for almost 200 years after it was founded. So the center of the spiral was filled with zeros. Thus, *The Women's Table* commented on the many years of discrimination against women at Yale.

80   In 1993, Lin completed remodeling a building to house the Museum of African Art in New York City. She also did a sculpture called *Groundswell* for Ohio State University.

    In 1994, Lin designed a 14-foot long clock for Pennsylvania Station in New York City. It is made of clear glass. It is lit by hundreds of fiber-optic points

85 of light.

    Lin has become an important American artist. Perhaps her greatest works are her monuments. They have helped heal the wounds of the Vietnam War and the civil rights struggle. Lin is still a young woman. She will no doubt have many more contributions to make to American art.

STEP 3: ASSESS IT

React

What did you learn from this article? Are you inspired at all? What do you think was Maya Lin's greatest work? Why?

Maya Lin is a renowned sculptor who gets asked to make many important monuments. Her work was largely criticized, but grew on people who visited the monument.

Check Your Strategy

Go back to the four predictions you made about the article on Maya Lin on page 4. Which of your predictions were right? Were some only partially right? On the lines below, check and comment on your predictions to reflect what you now know from reading the selection. An example is done for you.

SAMPLE PREDICTION: *This selection will be about how long it took Maya Lin to create the design for the Vietnam Veterans Memorial.*

SAMPLE CHECK: *There isn't any information in the article about how long it took Maya Lin to create the design. However, the contest was started in 1980 and the winner was announced in May of 1981. Lin traveled to Washington to study the building site, so it must have taken her a while to come up with the design. She also said at the beginning of the excerpt that the creative process sometimes takes a long time. So she must have designed the monument over a period of about six to eight months or so.*

Now check and comment on your own predictions on the lines below.

_____

_____

_____

_____

_____

Test-Taking Strategy

Many standardized tests ask you to read a statement and then decide if it is true or false. This testing method helps to check your comprehension of the article and your attention to some of the details. Look at the statements below. Circle **T** for the statements that are true. Circle **F** for the statements that are false.

1. Maya Lin was in her mid-60s when she designed the Vietnam Veterans Memorial.   T (F)

2. Lin's professor at college asked his students to enter designs for the Vietnam Veterans Memorial.   (T) F

3. Many Vietnam veterans were unhappy with the plans for the Vietnam Veterans Memorial.   (T) F

4. Lin was celebrated during the dedication ceremony in November 1982.   T (F)

5. Lin designed another memorial to commemorate the civil rights movement.   (T) F

6. Even though Lin designed several monuments, she never became famous.   T (F)

7. Lin's monument called "The Women's Table" is a comment on the many years women were not allowed at Yale University.   (T) F

8. Lin's work has helped people to heal wounds of painful chapters in U.S. history.   (T) F

STEP 4: THINK ABOUT IT

One of the most important tools in reading any nonfiction is **identifying the main idea** and the **supporting details.** Once you have done that, you can be sure that you understand what the article is about. Then you can begin to analyze and evaluate it.

Main Idea

The main idea is the most important idea of the paragraph or selection you are reading. Sometimes you will discover the main idea from the title of an article. At other times, sentences in the article will help you uncover the clues to find the main idea. Often, the first paragraph or the last paragraph of an article will give you clues about the main idea.

Sometimes writers do not state the main idea directly. Instead, they hint at the idea through the details in the selection. In these cases, you must **infer** the main idea from the details that are given. This means that you must gather evidence from the supporting details and then add them up to get the main idea. Instead of finding one sentence with the main idea, you have to put the main idea in your own words.

Supporting Details

Supporting details are sentences that help explain or support the main idea. They are related to the main idea in some way. Selections often have nonsupporting details, too. These are statements that may be interesting but are not directly related to the main idea.

Look at the statements below. Each one is a sentence or pair of sentences from the article on Maya Lin. One of the numbered statements represents the main idea of the article. That statement is a sentence that tells what the whole article is about. All the rest of the statements are supporting details that tell about the main idea. After each statement, write down **MI** for main idea or **SD** for supporting detail.

1. In 1980, a nationwide contest was held to design the Vietnam Veterans Memorial. One of Lin's professors asked the students in his class to enter designs. _____

2. Her design was called a "wall of shame." _____

3. In 1987, Lin was asked to design a memorial in Montgomery, Alabama, for those who had died in the civil rights struggle. _____

4. Maya Lin became one of the most controversial artists in the world. _____

5. "The Women's Table" commented on the many years of discrimination against women at Yale. _____

6. The Vietnam Veterans Memorial was dedicated on November 13, 1982. Lin's name was not even mentioned during the ceremony. _____

7. When the protesters found out that Lin was a Chinese-American woman, they were outraged. _____

8. The debate went on for nearly a year. Finally, a compromise was reached. The wall would be built as Lin had designed it. _____

Look at It Another Way

Another way to figure out the main idea is to create a chart like the one below. Using the statements from the activity above, fill in the chart so that you can see how the supporting details add up.

SD [ ]

+

SD [ ]

+

SD [ ]

MI [ ]

STEP 5: RELATE IT

1. Search the Internet to find copies of photographs of three or four monuments or buildings Maya Lin has designed. Download them and then study them. Finally, create a title for each piece that you think reflects the main idea of the building or monument. (Technology)

2. Using at least two Internet sources and two hard copy sources from the library, create an oral report on the monuments of Washington, D.C. Choose four or five monuments (or major buildings or statues) to focus on. Describe their message and their meaning for those who experience them. If you have visited Washington, you may want to include your firsthand account of the experience. Use photographs or drawings to enhance your talk. (Speaking/Listening)

3. Decide on an event in your life that you would like to memorialize. You may want to choose a time to celebrate—for example, when you did well at a sporting event, learned to drive, or celebrated a particular birthday. Or, you may choose a more solemn event to commemorate—such as the death of a loved one or another sad occasion. Draw the plans for a memorial for this event. Think about what material you would want the memorial to be made of. What color should it be? Most important, what message do you want it to convey to those who would see it? (Visual)

4. Visit a statue or a monument in your community. Take a pad of paper and pen with you and write a description of it. Be sure to include details such as what the memorial is made of, how big it is, and—most important—what message you feel it conveys to the observer. (Writing)

INTERVIEW

2

"ARNOLD SCHWARZENEGGER"
(from *American Dreams: Lost and Found* by Studs Terkel)

Learning Strategy:	Gathering Evidence from Text
Reading Skill:	Drawing Conclusions
Test-Taking Strategy:	Short Answer Synthesis

Setting the Scene

Almost all of your students will be familiar with Arnold Schwarzenegger as the mega-movie-star action hero of movies like *Eraser, Total Recall, Terminator,* and *True Lies.* Or, they may know him for his comedic movies like, *Twins, Jingle All the Way,* or *Kindergarten Cop.*

Arnold began his career as a bodybuilder in his native Austria. He was just seventeen when he picked up his first barbell. He discovered that girls loved men with muscles, and so he determined to be the "most pumped-up guy in the world." In just five years, he won his first championship, and by 1970 he was becoming a well-known figure in bodybuilding as he won his first Mr. Universe competition. He traveled to America in 1968, and as you will read from his interview, felt he had arrived at heaven on earth. He was obviously quite taken with everything American, and fit in well with life in Hollywood.

After winning six Mr. Olympia competitions—the highest honor for a body builder—Arnold retired from the sport. He soon came back, starring as himself in the movie *Pumping Iron.* Later he appeared in one more Mr. Olympia competition, and won—for the seventh time!

By then, Arnold was a household name. He was propelled to megastar status when he married Kennedy cousin Maria Shriver and was cast as the machine-gun wielding borg in *Terminator.*

Arnold has never stopped feeling the need to win, to compete, to achieve more. These days, he is acting—in both comedies and action movies—and he is pursuing his "activist" role as a spokesperson for the Inner City Games and for the Special Olympics. According to Arnold, he feels about giving to others the same as he does about winning: He says that everyone should "give as much as he can to help others."

Introducing the Skill

Drawing a conclusion means look at the evidence in front of you, consider your own knowledge of the subject, and then make a decision about what is happening. In many ways, drawing a conclusion is like making an inference, except that in drawing a conclusion, you use more of the evidence that you can see from the text or from the context.

You can introduce drawing conclusions by talking to students about how detectives solve a crime. Remind them that detectives gather clues from the scene, interview people who witnessed the crime, and then use their experience to make a decision about what has happened. You may want to lead students in a discussion about some local detective work that is in the news, or for fun, you may want to show them a mystery movie, such as an old Sherlock Holmes film.

If you don't have time to take a day to talk about drawing conclusions, use a photo or a picture to begin your lesson. Ask students to study the context of the photo or drawing and to draw conclusions about the setting, the time, the people, or the event shown. Make sure students support their conclusions with evidence from the visual text.

Especially for English Language Learners

Sharing Culture In his interview, Arnold Schwarzenegger talks about his affinity for Western philosophy as opposed to Eastern philosophy. Invite your class to discuss their perception of each of these philosophies. Ask your ELLs to talk about their perception of Western philosophy. Is this perception different from that of the native speakers?

Sharing Language In the interview, Arnold's words are taken verbatim, or word for word. There are a few places where he does not use English grammar in just the right context. Ask your ELLs to find these places and share them with the rest of the class. You will probably find that they will know the grammar sticking points better than their native speaking counterparts, having learned grammar more recently than the native speakers.

Assessing Understanding

On many tests, students will be asked to assess their understanding of a passage by analyzing it and by synthesizing their own prior knowledge with what they discover in the text. In this way, they will be using the reading skills of drawing conclusions and making inferences.

The questions asked in this section do not necessarily have a right or a wrong answer. However, there are clues that can point your students in the right direction. Go over these questions very carefully and model for students the way that they might find the answer (see **Step 4: Think About It**). Explain to students that learning how to apply these skills will help them when they take tests. It will also help them beyond the classroom, as they think critically about what they read later when they are developing skills for the real world.

Reading Further

The New Encyclopedia of Modern Bodybuilding by Arnold Schwarzenegger, Bill Dobbins (contributor), Fireside.

Arnold: The Education of a Bodybuilder by Arnold Schwarzenegger, Douglas Kent, contributor, Fireside.

True Myths: The Life and Times of Arnold Schwarzenegger by Nigel Andrews, Birch Lane Press.

Extending to Technology

To find more information, use the following terms to conduct on-line searches: Arnold Schwarzenegger, bodybuilding, and Mr. Universe. Or visit these web sites:
www.schwarzenegger.com
www.Austria.com

INTERVIEW

"ARNOLD SCHWARZENEGGER"
(from *American Dreams: Lost and Found* by Studs Terkel)

Learning Strategy:	Gathering Evidence from Text
Reading Skill:	Drawing Conclusions
Test-Taking Strategy:	Short Answer Synthesis

STEP 1: LINK IT

Before You Read

Have you ever heard the expression *the American Dream?* What does that phrase mean to you? For many, this expression means living a comfortable life, being highly successful, owning a home, perhaps raising a family.

The expression *American Dream* originated when the United States was still a young nation. It became popular during the mid- to late-1800s and early 1900s when immigrants were leaving their homelands with hopes of making a "better" life. This "better" life included many possibilities for success—money, land, freedom, and ultimately, comfort. The growth of the cities to the west of America's East Coast—like Chicago and Detroit—with all of their industry and possibility of making it rich became a symbol of the American Dream.

But for many of these newcomers flocking to the industrial centers in the United States, the American Dream turned to an ugly reality. Workers realized that they were not earning enough to pay their monthly bills. Immigrants were treated without respect. Only a handful of people succeeded in achieving the ultimate picture of the American Dream. Yet the pursuit of the dream continued, and continues still. People still look at the United States as a place of possibility. Anything is possible in the United States. But is it? What do you think?

In the interview you are about to read, you will meet a famous actor before he became famous. You will meet a much younger Arnold Schwarzenegger long before he ever uttered "Hasta la vista, baby," or "I'll be back." The man you are going to meet spoke to interviewer Studs Terkel, who made a career out of asking questions that invited people to reveal their innermost selves.

This interview with Arnold Schwarzenegger was published in 1980 along with interviews of 99 other people from all over the country. Studs Terkel had asked each of them about what they dreamed of. The book, *American Dreams: Lost and Found,* shows us these 100 people—from Miss America to a rural farmer to a rich businessman to a small store owner—all have a dream of changing their lives and finding something better for themselves and their children.

As you read this piece spoken by Arnold Schwarzenegger and recorded by Studs Terkel, think about how much you agree or disagree with Arnold Schwarzenegger. Do you have anything in common with him as a young, aspiring man? Then think about what you know about Arnold Schwarzenegger today. Do you think he has achieved his dream? What do you think might be Arnold's next dream?

Set a Strategy

A little later in this lesson, you are going to learn how to **draw a conclusion** about Arnold Schwarzenegger's character. Drawing a conclusion means that you **gather evidence,** and then add it to your own **prior knowledge** to make a decision about something. Here's a simple example: You go to someone's house and notice that they have dishes of water and food on the floor. (This is the evidence.) You know from experience that people—maybe you—put dishes on the floor to give pets water to drink and food to eat. (That's your prior knowledge.) You then draw the conclusion that the people you are visiting probably have pets. (That's your conclusion.)

You can't draw a conclusion without gathering clues. This is where reading can be a little like being a detective. You look for a clue directly stated in the text to tell you about a character or an event or an idea. Then you analyze or evaluate those clues based on information you already have from life experience. Finally, you add those two things together to draw a conclusion.

As you read this interview with Arnold Schwarzenegger, look for clues that tell you about his character. You might find clues about his character by reading about what he feels is important in life. You might also find clues about his character by analyzing how he reacts to various situations. As you ask yourself questions about character, look for clues in the interview that stand out. What is Arnold's idea of the American Dream? Be sure that when you are asked a question and you answer it you can back up your answer with specific clues in the text.

Set a Purpose

Remember to ask yourself the important "purpose" questions. The first is **What kind of writing is this?** You know that the excerpt is an interview because it says so in the lesson heading. What exactly is an interview and when are you likely to come across it in your reading?

Interviews are question-and-answer sessions. You probably listen to spoken interviews all the time. Television programs are full of them—from serious interviews on the morning news shows, to funny interviews on the late night talk shows, to something in-between on the afternoon variety shows. What makes a *good* interview?

Some interviews are important and require close listening or reading. Most news stories in newspapers and magazines are the result of interviews. The people being interviewed in these stories need to be very concise in their answers. Some interviews are not particularly serious, such as an interview with a celebrity. In that case, you can read the interview fairly lightly, skimming for information.

Then there are interviews like the one you are about to read. It is an interview with a celebrity, but this interview is a little different. First, it is conducted by one of the greatest interviewers of all time, Studs Terkel. In this case, Terkel asked Arnold Schwarzenegger to talk about himself and about his dreams. You will want to read this interview fairly closely. It not only reflects a lot about an interesting celebrity, but it also jogs us to think about our own dreams and backgrounds and how much alike or different we are from Schwarzenegger. Jot down your answer to the second "purpose" question: **Why am I reading this?**

_____

_____

_____

_____

_____

_____

STEP 2: READ IT

In this short interview we learn a lot about a current legend—Arnold Schwarzenegger. By simply asking the "right" question, Studs Terkel is able to draw out a lot about Schwarzenegger, the bodybuilder, before he became a movie star. What do you think Arnold reveals most about his character?

Call me Arnold.

I was born in a little Austrian town, outside Graz. It was a 300-year-old house. When I was ten years old, I had the dream of being the best in the world in something. When I was fifteen, I had a dream that I wanted to be the best body
5 builder in the world and the most muscular man. It was not only a dream I dreamed at night. It was also a daydream. It was so much in my mind that I felt it had to become a reality. It took me five years of hard work. Five years later, I turned this dream into reality and became Mr. Universe, the best-built man in the world.

10 "Winning" is a very important word. There is one that achieves what he wanted to achieve and there are hundreds of thousands that failed. It singles you out: the winner.

I came out second three times, but that is not what I call losing. The bottom line for me was: Arnold has to be the winner. I have to win more often the Mr.
15 Universe title than anybody else. I won it five times consecutively. I hold the record as Mr. Olympia, the top professional body-building championship. I won it six times. That's why I retired. There was nobody even close to me. Everybody gave up competing against me. That's what I call a winner.

When I was a small boy, my dream was not to be big physically, but big in a
20 way that everybody listens to me when I talk, that I'm a very important person, that people recognize me and see me as something special. I had a big need for being singled out.

Also my dream was to end up in America. When I was ten years old, I dreamed of being an American. At the time I didn't know much about America, just that it
25 was a wonderful country. I felt it was where I belonged. I didn't like being in a little country like Austria. I did everything possible to get out. I did so in 1968, when I was twenty-one years old.

If I would believe in life after death, I would say my before-life I was living in America. That's why I feel so good here. It is the country where you can turn

30 your dream into reality. Other countries don't have those things. When I came over here to America, I felt I was in heaven. In America, we don't have an obstacle. Nobody's holding you back.

Number One in America pretty much takes care of the rest of the world. You kind of run through the rest of the world like nothing. I'm trying to make people

35 in America aware that they should appreciate what they have here. You have the best tax advantages here and the best prices here and the best products here.

One of the things I always had was a business mind. When I was in high school, a majority of my classes were business classes. Economics and accounting and mathematics. When I came over here to this country I really didn't speak

40 English almost at all. I learned English and then started taking business courses, because that's what America is known for: business. Turning one dollar into a million dollars in a short period of time. Also when you make money, how do you keep it?

That's one of the most important things when you have money in your hand,

45 how can you keep it? Or make more out of it? Real estate is one of the best ways of doing that. I own apartment buildings, office buildings, and raw land. That's my love, real estate.

I have emotions. But what you do, you keep them cold or you store them away for a time. You must control your emotions, you must have command over your-

50 self. Three, four months before a competition, I could not be interfered by other people's problems. This is sometimes called selfish. It's the only way you can be if you want to achieve something. Any emotional things inside me, I try to keep cold so it doesn't interfere with my training.

Many times things really touched me. I felt them and I felt sensitive about

55 them. But I had to talk myself out of it. I had to suppress those feelings in order to go on. Sport is one of those activities where you really have to concentrate. You must pay attention a hundred percent to the particular thing you're doing. There must be nothing else on your mind. Emotions must not interfere. Otherwise, you're thinking about your girlfriend. You're in love, your positive energies get

60 channeled into another direction rather than going into your weight room or making money.

You have to choose at a very early date what you want: a normal life or to achieve things you want to achieve. I never wanted to win a popularity contest in doing things the way people want me to do it. I went the road I thought was best
65 for me. A few people thought I was cold, selfish. Later they found out that's not the case. After I achieve my goal, I can be Mr. Nice Guy. You know what I mean?

California is to me a dreamland. It is the absolute combination of everything I was always looking for. It has all the money in the world there, show business there, wonderful weather there, beautiful country, ocean is there. Snow skiing in
70 the winter, you can go in the desert the same day. You have beautiful-looking people there. They all have a tan.

I believe very strongly in the philosophy of staying hungry. If you have a dream and it becomes a reality, don't stay satisfied with it too long. Make up a new dream and hunt after that one and turn it into reality. When you have that dream
75 achieved, make up a new dream.

I am a strong believer in Western philosophy, the philosophy of success, of progress, of getting rich. The Eastern philosophy is passive, which I believe in maybe three percent of the times, and the ninety-seven percent is Western, conquering and going on. It's a beautiful philosophy, and America should keep
80 it up.

STEP 3: ASSESS IT

React

What is your immediate reaction to this interview? Did you like it? Were you bored by it? Did you learn anything from it? What is the most interesting part?

_____

_____

_____

_____

_____

_____

Check Your Understanding

Read the following questions and then choose the best answer for each.

1. From what country is Arnold from originally?
   - a. Switzerland
   - b. Austria
   - c. France
   - d. Germany

2. How long did it take Arnold to realize his dream of becoming Mr. Universe?
   - a. two years
   - b. six months
   - c. six years
   - d. five years

3. What does Arnold say that America is best known for?
   - a. bodybuilding
   - b. business
   - c. movie stars with tans
   - d. feeling free with your emotions

4. What does Arnold feel is the most important thing about being a winner?
   - a. It singles you out as the best.
   - b. It makes you rich and probably famous.
   - c. It means you get great tax advantages.
   - d. It helps you be better at business.

Check Your Strategy

There are several places where Arnold doesn't come right out and tell you something. But you can draw conclusions based on evidence and your prior knowledge. Answer the questions below by drawing conclusions from the article. You may need to refer to the text.

1. What kind of student do you think Arnold was? _____

   _____

2. Do you think it would be intimidating to face Arnold as a competitor? Why or why not? _____

   _____

   _____

3. Do you think Arnold would make a good teacher or trainer to those working to be bodybuilders? Why or why not? _____

   _____

   _____

Test-Taking Strategy

On many tests, you will be asked to analyze something that you have read and synthesize it with information you already know. This means that you will be asked to explain what a passage means and in what way it is significant. You will be using several reading skills to answer questions like these—including drawing conclusions, which you'll analyze in the next step.

Read the following passages and then answer the questions that follow. You may refer to the text if you need some help. When you are done, trade papers with a partner and then compare your answers.

1. "I believe very strongly in the philosophy of staying hungry." What do you think Arnold means by this statement? _____

   _____

   _____

2. Why do you think Arnold says that if he believed in life after death, he would say that his "before-life I was living in America?" _____

_____

_____

3. Arnold says, "You have to choose at a very early date what you want: a normal life or to achieve things you want to achieve." What do you think Arnold means by a "normal life"? _____

_____

_____

4. Arnold said that he is "a strong believer in Western philosophy, philosophy of success, of progress, of getting rich." Do you agree with him that these things reflect the Western philosophy? What does the Western philosophy mean to you? _____

_____

_____

STEP 4: THINK ABOUT IT

Look at your answer for the third question above. It asked you to discuss what you think Arnold means by a "normal life." This question asked you to **draw a conclusion**. A conclusion, in this case, is a decision or a judgment that you make after you have carefully examined important information.

Drawing Conclusions

Earlier you learned about gathering evidence to help you draw a conclusion. Let's look closely at how you can apply the reading strategy of drawing conclusions to the question about a normal life.

First, you read the question: "Arnold says, 'You have to choose at a very early date what you want: a normal life or to achieve things you want to achieve.' What do you think Arnold means by a 'normal life'?"

Gathering Evidence

Second, you go to the text and **gather evidence** that might help you answer this question:

Nowhere specifically does Arnold say what he thinks is a normal life. But he talks about his homeland as a very small place. At line 25, he says, "I felt it (America) was where I belonged. I didn't like being in a little country like Austria. I did everything possible to get out." This hints to me that he feels Austria is too small for him. Later he says, "It (America) is the country where you can turn your dream into reality. Other countries don't have those things." So from this I gather that Arnold felt that he couldn't realize his dream in Austria. He says that there is no obstacle in America. So he must have felt there were obstacles in Austria. Arnold also says that he has emotions, but he suppresses his feelings so he can reach his goal. He probably thinks of "normal" people as people who can live day in and day out with their emotions. He also says that after he achieves his goal, he can be Mr. Nice Guy. I think this means that he believes that "normal" also means nice.

Do you see how we gathered clues directly from the text? Now you try it. Reread your answer to the first question from the exercise on page 24:

"I believe very strongly in the philosophy of staying hungry." What do you think Arnold means by this statement?

Now write the clues from the text that led you to your answer.

_____

_____

_____

_____

_____

_____

Look at It Another Way

Another way to look at drawing conclusions is to create a web so that it is easier to visualize what you're reading. Sometimes we draw conclusions and we're not quite sure how we did it. That's where the evidence comes in. Let's look again at the question from **Assess It** about leading a normal life. Here's how the evidence might look in a web.

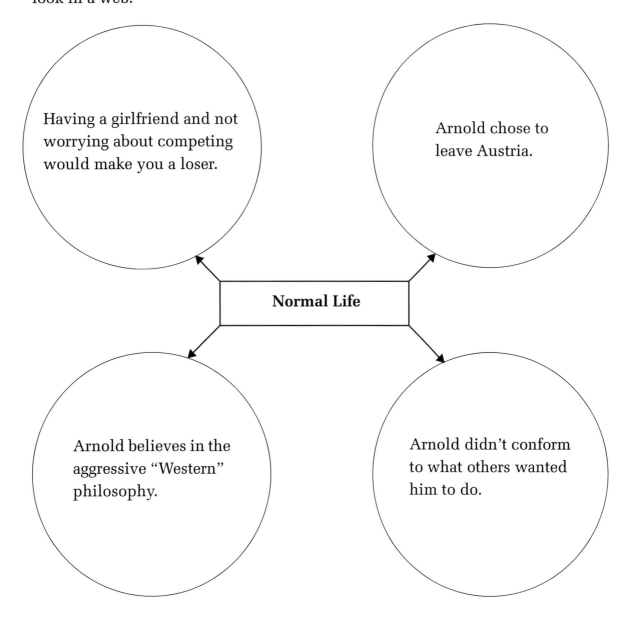

STEP 5: RELATE IT

1. Since his interview with Studs Terkel, Arnold Schwarzenegger married well-known commentator Maria Shriver, and Arnold is now the father of four children. As you know, he has also become a very successful actor. Using the Internet, television, or a computerized periodical search in the library, find an interview with Arnold Schwarzenegger from within the last five years. Can you find any evidence that his values or dreams have changed? (Technology)

2. Bodybuilding continues to be a very specialized sport around the world. Find out about this sport and what the criteria are for winning the Mr. Universe or Mr. Olympia competition. Remember that bodybuilding is not just for men, either! Create a chart that outlines some of the steps a person would need to take to become a professional bodybuilder. You may want to include the names of some of the more well-known bodybuilders. (Visual)

3. Conduct your own miniature version of Studs Terkel's *American Dreams: Lost and Found*. Interview various people from your school (include staff, teachers, and other students) and ask them about their dreams for the future. You could also interview people outside of school. Look for a broad cross section of occupations, countries of origin, education, and age. Record your interviews by taking notes or using a tape recorder (with your subject's permission). Then present your interview to the rest of the class. Remember to ask open questions that will invite your subjects to say more about themselves than just a few phrases. (Speaking/Listening)

4. Write your own journal entry about your dreams and aspirations. What do you find you have in common with Arnold Schwarzenegger? What things are different? Do you think that money and show business and wonderful weather are the most important things in life? Do you think that Arnold was just swept up in the idea of the "possibility" of realizing his dream? (Writing)

ON-LINE RESEARCH ARTICLE

3

"RAP"
(by Robert Bowman, from *Encarta Online Encyclopedia*)

Learning Strategy:	Finding Context Clues
Reading Skill:	Making Generalizations
Test-Taking Strategy:	Understanding Main Idea and Details

Setting the Scene

Undoubtedly, most of your students will be familiar with rap music, although some may not. You may want to bring in a recording or listen through the Web in class to a couple of different rap practitioners. As you introduce the lesson on rap music, engage the students in a discussion about their reactions to it, why they like it, why they don't like it, what artists they favor, which they do not. Ask them to talk about the message that rap music gives to them. What part of American culture does it reflect to them? Ask them to discuss what they know about the history of rap music or what details they know about the life of various rappers. As you discuss, be sure to share your own thoughts about rap music.

Introducing the Skill

This lesson builds on the information learned in Lesson 1 on main idea and supporting details. In this lesson, students will be learning to identify context clues, and they will be learning to look for and make generalizations. Both of these skills are key to understanding better what they read.

The entry from the *Encarta Online Encyclopedia* is not easy reading. Let students know, however, that when they do on-line research, this is the level of reading that they will encounter. Encourage students to skim the selection before they read it to identify the boldfaced words that they may not know. You may want to preview these words in more depth to help their reading go smoothly. Explain to students that this process of skimming for unfamiliar words may be a good way to get started when they read any on-line research article.

Students will also be looking for and making generalizations. This instruction will help them recognize a generalization and decide if it is valid or faulty based on evidence from the text and evidence from their own experience. Emphasize that students' experience is a very important part of their reading. It helps them to decide if things ring true or not—and it is this experience that ultimately helps them build their knowledge base. Be sure to carry this model forward in future lessons and in other subject areas so that students will continue to understand and make generalizations.

Especially for English Language Learners

Sharing Culture Students will learn that rap music is a genre that has greatly influenced black and white culture in North America.

Teacher Guide

Ask your English language learners if there is a musical form like rap that has had the same sort of impact in their country of origin. Encourage your ELLs to bring in an example of music that has influenced their culture. Invite your ELLs to lead a discussion on the way that music reflects the spirit or psyche of a particular culture. Look for commonalties among your native speakers and your ELLs and point them out as the discussion unfolds.

Sharing Language Go over the slang words in the selection (*rap, dis, fly, chill, gansta rap, wack*) and explain what these words mean. Also, invite your native speakers and your ELLs to pair up as they read the article. In some cases, your native speakers will be able to help define some of the words, and, in other cases, your ELLs may have enough knowledge of English roots to help figure out what the words mean.

Assessing Understanding

One of the most common standardized tests is the multiple-choice format. Explain to students that this kind of a test is intended to help them recall and test their comprehension of what they have read.

Teach students to first eliminate answers they are sure are wrong when working in a multiple-choice test. Then students have to make a choice among the answers they think may be right. One way to help students prepare for these tests is to invite students to create tests themselves, seeking out the information they feel is important to be tested on. This way they can practice culling the main ideas and the essential supporting details.

Remind students of formats where they might see multiple-choice questions being asked, such as questionnaires or even television quiz shows such as "Who Wants to Be a Millionaire?"

Reading Further

Black Noise: Rap Music and Black Culture in Contemporary America by Tricia Rose, Wesleyan University Press.

Droppin Science: Critical Essays on Rap Music and Hip-Hop Culture by William E. Perkins, Editor, Temple University Press.

Extending to Technology

To find more information on-line, use the following search terms: rap music, hip-hop, and individual rap artists. Or, visit these web sites:

www.busboy.sped.ukans.edu
www.rapdict.org
www.rapreviews.com

ON-LINE RESEARCH ARTICLE

"RAP"
(by Robert Bowman, from *Encarta Online Encyclopedia*)

Learning Strategy:	Finding Context Clues
Reading Skill:	Making Generalizations
Test-Taking Strategy:	Understanding Main Idea and Details

STEP 1: LINK IT

Before You Read

What is your favorite type of music? Is it rock, classical, folk, jazz, reggae, rap? Why do you like to listen to a particular kind of music? Does it remind you of something or someone? Does it put you in a certain mood? Do you know the words and sing along? Or do you put the music on and have it as background to whatever you are doing? Perhaps you play an instrument or play in a band—if so, how do you feel when you play music?

You are about to read an article from the Internet about rap music. As you will read, rap music began in one section of New York City and spread to neighborhoods all over the country. Now rap has joined the ranks of popular culture. Almost everyone is at least familiar with its sound, if not with specific artists and songs. There is a whole culture that goes with rap music—clothes, slang expressions, and even art. Rap music is thought by many to be a voice for those who are not part of mainstream culture in the United States—particularly those from the country's inner cities. As you read, think about your own favorite music and what it says about you. How does your favorite music reflect your thoughts, feelings, and culture?

Set a Strategy

You are about to read an entry from *Encarta Online Encyclopedia,* part of the World Wide Web. The entry on rap music is typical of Internet research articles in that it is written at a high level of reading.

The vocabulary is challenging, and you may not know all of the words. As you read, you will find words that are in bold type with blank lines after them. These bold words are the harder words. You will have to do one of two things to discover their meaning. One thing you can do is look the words up in the dictionary. There you will find one or more definitions printed next to the word, and you will have to decide which meaning best fits the word and makes sense in the article. Another thing you can do is to look at the words around the unfamiliar words for hints about what the word might mean. This process is called using **context clues.** *Context* means the words that come before or after an unknown word that can help determine its meaning.

Let's look at an example from the article you are about to read: "Defenders of gangsta rap argue that no matter who is listening to the music, the raps are justified because they accurately **portray** life in inner-city America." Here's how you might figure out what the word *portray* means if you don't already know:

> *When I read the word* portray, *I'm not completely sure what it means. But I can use the rest of the sentence to try to figure it out through context clues. The sentence says that rap has defenders, which suggests that there must be people who don't like or are attacking rap music. These defenders are saying that even though there are attackers, rap is a good idea, because it does something (portrays life) in inner-city America. It makes sense that rap is a good thing if it shows what life is like in the inner city. So therefore,* portray *must mean "show."*

As you read, try to figure out what the words in bold type mean by using context clues. In some cases, you should be able to figure it out. In other cases, you may not be able to figure the words out. Don't worry, though; all of the words are defined in a glossary at the end of the selection. But first try to guess the meaning and write it in the blank space next to the boldfaced word.

Set a Purpose

Remember you learned about setting a purpose for reading. Remember to ask the two important questions:

What kind of writing is this? _____

Why am I reading this?

_____

_____

_____

_____

If you answered "informational writing" or "factual writing" for the first question you would be right. Only you can answer the second question, but hopefully you said something like "to learn more about rap music," "to find out where rap music began," "to learn about the first rappers," or "to understand some of the reasons people like rap music."

STEP 2: READ IT

This article from Encarta Online Encyclopedia *is intended to give information and background about rap music. If you were doing a report on rap music, the on-line encyclopedia is one of the first places you would look to get information. You will note that this entry is full of facts that include where rap began and how it has taken hold in American culture. You will also learn about some of the people who first made rap popular. This article was written by Robert M. Bowman, Assistant Professor of Music at York University in England. He won a Grammy award in 1995 for Best Album Notes for* The Complete Stax/Volt Soul Singles, Volume 3: 1972–1975.

    Rap, genre of rhythm-and-blues music (R&B) that consists of rhythmic vocals **declaimed** _____ over musical accompaniment. The accompaniment generally consists of electronic drum beats combined with *samples* (digitally isolated sound bites) from other musical recordings. The first rap recording

5 was made in 1979 and the genre rose to **prominence** _____ in the United States in the mid-1980s. Although the term *rap* is often used **interchangeably** _____ with *hip-hop,* the **latter** _____ term encompasses the subculture that rap music is simply one part of. The term *hip-hop* **derives** _____ from one of the earliest phrases used in rap, and

10 can be found on the **seminal** _____ recording "Rapper's Delight" (1979) by Sugarhill Gang. In addition to rap music, the hip-hop subculture also **comprises** _____ other forms of expression, including break dancing and **graffiti** _____ art as well as a unique slang vocabulary and fashion sense.

15   Rap originated in the mid-1970s in the South Bronx area of New York City. The rise of rap in many ways parallels the birth of rock and roll in the 1950s (*see* Rock Music: *Rock and Roll*): Both originated within the African American community and both were initially recorded by small, independent record labels and musicians, a few of whom began performing it. For rock and roll it was a

20 white American from Mississippi, Elvis Presley, who broke into the *Billboard* magazine popular music charts. For rap it was a white group from New York, the Beastie Boys. Their release "(You Gotta) Fight for Your Right (To Party!)" (1986) was one of the first two rap records to reach the *Billboard* top-ten list of popular

hits. The other significant early rap recording to reach the top ten, "Walk This

25 Way" (1986), was a **collaboration** _____ of the black rap group
Run-DMC and the white **hard-rock** _____ band Aerosmith. Soon
after 1986, the use of samples and declaimed vocal styles became widespread in
the popular music of both black and white performers, significantly altering
previous notions of what constitutes a **legitimate** _____ song,

30 composition, or musical instrument.

Rap music originated as a cross-cultural product. Most of its important early
practitioners—including Kool Herc, D.J. Hollywood, and Afrika Bambaataa—
were either first- or second- generation Americans of Caribbean ancestry. Herc

35 and Hollywood are both credited with introducing the Jamaican style of cutting
and mixing into the musical culture of the South Bronx. By most accounts Herc
was the first **DJ** _____ to buy two copies of the same record for just
a 15-second *break* (rhythmic instrumental segment) in the middle. By mixing
back and forth between the two copies he was able to double, triple, or indefi-

40 nitely extend the break. In so doing, Herc effectively deconstructed and recon-
structed so-called found sound, using the **turntable** _____ as a
musical instrument.

While he was cutting with two turntables, Herc would also perform with the
microphone in Jamaican toasting style—joking, boasting, and using myriad in-

45 group references. Herc's musical parties eventually gained **notoriety**
_____ and were often documented on cassette tapes that were
recorded with the relatively new **boombox** _____, or blaster, technology. Taped **duplicates** _____ of these parties rapidly made their
way through the Bronx, Brooklyn, and uptown Manhattan, **spawning**

50 _____ a number of similar DJ acts. Among the new breed of DJs was
Afrika Bambaataa, the first important Black Muslim in rap. (The Muslim pres-
ence would become very influential in the late 1980s.) Bambaataa often engaged
in sound-system battles with Herc, similar to the so-called cutting contests in
jazz a generation earlier. The sound system competitions were held at city parks,

55 where **hot-wired** _____ street lamps supplied electricity, or at local
clubs. Bambaataa sometimes mixed sounds from rock-music recordings and

Name: **Student Page**

television shows into the standard **funk** _____ and **disco**
_____ fare that Herc and most of his followers relied upon. By
using rock records, Bambaataa extended rap beyond the immediate reference

60 points of contemporary black youth culture. By the 1990s any sound source was
considered **fair game** _____ and rap artists borrowed sounds from
such **disparate** _____ sources as Israeli folk music, bebop jazz
records, and television news broadcasts.

In 1976 Grandmaster Flash introduced the technique of quick mixing, in

65 which **sound bites** _____ as short as one or two seconds are
combined for a **collage** _____ effect. Quick mixing paralleled the
rapid-editing style of television advertising used at the time. Shortly after Flash
introduced quick mixing, his partner Grandmaster Melle Mel composed the first
extended stories in rhymed rap. Up to this point, most of the words heard over

70 the work of disc jockeys such as Herc, Bambaataa, and Flash had been improvised phrases and expressions. In 1978 DJ Grand Wizard Theodore introduced
the technique of scratching to produce rhythmic patterns.

Since the mid-1980s rap music has greatly influenced both black and white

75 culture in North America. Much of the slang hip-hop culture, including such
terms as *dis, fly, def, chill,* and *wack,* have become standard parts of the vocabulary of a significant number of young people of various ethnic origins. Many rap
enthusiasts **assert** _____ that rap functions as a voice for a community without access to the **mainstream** _____ media. According to

80 **advocates** _____, rap serves to **engender** _____ self-
pride, self-help, and self-improvement, communicating a positive and fulfilling
sense of black history that is largely absent from other American institutions. . . .
Gangsta rap has also been severely criticized for lyrics that many people interpret
as glorifying the most violent and *misogynist* (woman-hating) imagery in the

85 history of popular music. The style's popularity with middle-class whites has
been attacked as vicarious thrill-seeking of the most insidious sort. Defenders
of gangsta rap argue that no matter who is listening to the music, the raps are
justified because they accurately **portray** _____ life in inner-city
America.

STEP 3: ASSESS IT

Check Your Purpose

Go back to your answers to the question **Why am I reading this?** What reasons did you come up with before you read? Did you find the answers you were looking for? What new information did you discover from your reading that you didn't write down before you read?

_____

_____

_____

Check Your Strategy

How did you do with uncovering clues about the meanings of the boldfaced words? Working with a small group or a partner, check your definitions against the definitions below and see how well you did. Remember to use the context clue strategy whenever you come across a word you do not know. Doublecheck the words in a dictionary so that you can see how they are pronounced.

declaimed: uttered or spoken

prominence: the state of being easily seen; famous, important

interchangeably: something that can be exchanged or substituted for another

latter: refers to the last thing just mentioned; in the article, *the latter* refers to *hip-hop*. People use the phrase *the latter* so they don't have to repeat the word that was just spoken or written.

derives: is taken or received from a source; comes from. In the article, the word *derives* means that the term *hip-hop* comes from an early rap song.

seminal: the source or the origin. When the article refers to "Rapper's Delight" as a seminal recording, it means that that song is the original, the first, the source of rap.

comprises: consists of or includes; is made up of

graffiti: art or words that are scratched onto a wall

collaboration: the act of working together toward a common goal

hard-rock: a subgenre of music that emerged in the 1960s focusing on thick layers of sound, loud volume levels, and virtuoso guitar solos

legitimate: conforming to standard rules or accepted standards

DJ: stands for Disc Jockey—a person who plays music and hosts music programs at a radio station or party

turntable: a rotating platform that plays a record album

notoriety: fame; the condition of being well-known or widely commented upon by the public

boombox: a radio and/or sound system with speakers often played very loudly

duplicates: doubles or copies

spawning: bringing forth, leading to

hot-wired: something that runs on electricity stolen from another source

funk: a variant of soul music that was influenced by rock. Many of the funk sounds were derived from African rhythms with long, improvised solos.

disco: another genre of rock with a simple beat, great for dance rhythms

fair game: anything goes, there are no rules that make something a "fair game." In this article, it means that any sound source could be used.

disparate: unequal or unalike; having nothing in common

sound bites: short recordings of sound, often from a news event or program

collage: an assembly of different pieces of art or, in this case, sound, to make one picture or sound

assert: to say something positively or definitely

mainstream: something that is part of accepted popular culture; something everyone is familiar with

advocates: stands up for, supports publicly

engender: to cause to exist or happen

portray: show

Test-Taking Strategy

On many standardized tests, you will be asked to recall the main idea and important supporting details from an article you read using a multiple-choice format as on page 39. In Lesson 1, you learned how to find the main idea and supporting details.

First, answer the multiple-choice questions on the next page to be sure that you understood the main idea and supporting details from the article. Then, create your own multiple-choice test with five more questions about the article. (Be sure you know the answers to the questions you ask!) Once you have created the test, trade papers with a partner and then fill in the answers. Then trade back and correct each other's paper. Discuss any of the answers you got wrong and go back to the text to find the right answers.

Circle the correct answer for each of the questions below:

1. Rap is part of what genre?
   a. classical music
   b. rhythm and blues
   c. jazz
   d. hip-hop

2. Rap originated in what American city?
   a. San Francisco, California
   b. Brooklyn, New York
   c. South Bronx, New York
   d. Chicago, Illinois

3. Most of the first rap practitioners were of what ancestry?
   a. African
   b. Asian
   c. Canadian
   d. Caribbean

4. Quick mixing is
   a. cooking to the beat of rap music
   b. combining jazz and classical
   c. combining one- or two-second sound bites to make a collage effect
   d. using a turntable as a musical instrument

5. Gangsta rap has been criticized for
   a. its offbeat rhythm
   b. its violent and misogynist imagery
   c. its popularity with middle-class whites
   d. its accurate portrayal of life in inner-city America

6. The main idea of this article is
   a. Rap began in 1979.
   b. In 1976 Grandmaster Flash introduced the technique of quick mixing.
   c. Early rap practitioners were Americans of Caribbean ancestry.
   d. Rap music has greatly influenced culture in the United States.

STEP 4: THINK ABOUT IT

When you read nonfiction articles like the one you just read, it is useful to connect new information to what you already know. This way you can build your knowledge base and continue to add more information. Doing this can help you remember what you read. It can also help you better understand what you read.

Identifying and Making Generalizations

It is important to be able to **identify** and **make generalizations.** A generalization is a broad judgment or conclusion. It is a statement that is usually and universally true. Identifying generalizations will help you evaluate what you read. Making generalizations will enable you to apply what you read to other situations, in class, or in life.

Here are some examples of generalizations:

All people need food to live.

Most fire engines are red.

Both of these statements are universally true. They are both based on facts. How do you know they are generalizations? First, you must find the key words that tell you it is a generalization. Second, you must use your own experience and knowledge to determine if the generalization is true. And third, you must ask yourself some important questions so that you can make your own generalization based on what you read.

Look for Key Words

The first step in making a generalization is to look for key words in the article you are reading. A generalization is usually being made when you see the word or words *all, none, never, every, always, many, most, in many ways, sometimes, often, usually, generally, typically,* or *occasionally.*

Here are some examples:

***Every** child deserves to be treated with love and respect.* (This is universally true. There are no exceptions.)

***Many** birds leave New England and fly south for the winter.* (This means that many, but not all, the New England birds fly south.)

*Children should **never** be allowed to play with matches.* (There is no time when it is a good idea for children to play with matches.)

***Most** city orchestras are made up of professional musicians.* (However, it is still possible that there may be some city orchestras who have amateur musicians.)

*The weather in Florida is **typically** hot from May through September.* (There may be some days between May and September when the weather is cool.)

Here's one from the article you just read about rap music:

*The rise of rap **in many ways** parallels the birth of rock and roll.* (Rap and rock and roll have many things in common about how they got started, but not all things in common.)

Combine New Evidence and Prior Knowledge

The second step in making a generalization is to gather evidence from what you have read and combine it with your own prior knowledge to decide if the generalization is true. For example, if you read the sentence ***All** fire engines are red,* you would know that the statement is untrue because you have seen fire engines that are yellow and lime green. If you read the sentence ***Most** fire engines are red,* you would know that indeed there are some fire engines that are red, but there are also some fire engines that are other colors. But you could still say that the generalization is right, since **most** fire engines that you know of are red.

Ask the Questions

The third step in making generalizations is to ask yourself questions about what you have read. Here are the questions:

1. What is the generalization that the author is making?
2. What evidence does the author use to make this generalization?
3. Is that evidence reliable?
4. What do I already know about this subject?
5. What universal truth can I gather from this statement?

Here's an example of how you might think about a statement from the article on rap:

"Much of the slang of hip-hop culture, including such terms as *dis, fly, def, chill,* and *wack,* have become standard parts of the vocabulary of a significant number of young people of various ethnic origins."

*I'll ask myself the questions: 1. **What generalization is the author making?** Well, first of all, he's saying that many slang expressions come directly from rap or hip-hop culture. 2. **What evidence does he give?** He talked earlier about some of the first recordings of rap music, and he says that hip-hop subculture includes other forms of expression like fashion, graffiti, and unique slang words. 3. **Is the evidence reliable?** I think that this is very reliable information because it comes from an on-line* *encyclopedia and the article is written by a music professor. 4.* **What do I already know about this subject?** *Even though I don't know exactly what all of the words the author uses as examples mean, I have heard* dis *and* chill *and* wack *on a couple of rap songs I know. So my own experience helps me to believe that the author is correct. 5.* **What universal truth can I get from this?** *I can say definitely that these slang words originated in rap and hip-hop and that they are a significant part of our culture.*

Look at It Another Way

Another way to look at making generalizations is to create a chart or a web to help you answer the important questions. In the middle of the web below, there is a statement from the rap article. Around it are the five questions. Use a web like this to help you organize your thoughts as you read for generalizations.

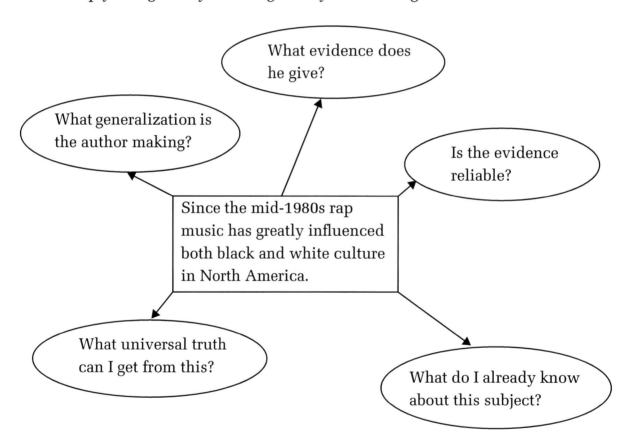

Steps to Successful Reading: Nonfiction

STEP 5: RELATE IT

1. Listen to a rap song and see how many influences you can find that crop up in the song. Are there television newscasts? Jazz? Bebop? Write an article analyzing the rap song you chose. (Writing)

2. Choose one of the early rap performers and listen to his or her music. See if you can pick out any of the slang expressions that you read about in the article (*dis, fly, wack, chill*). Once you have listened to the whole song, make a generalization about whether the song has a positive or negative message. Gather clues from the lyrics and jot them down. You may want to listen to the song more than once. (Auditory)

3. Select two well-known rap musicians and research them on the Internet. See how many facts you can gather about their lives and musical work. What do they have in common? What is different? Make a chart that includes the name of each musician at the top. Then list hometown, influences, band instruments, song subjects, and anything else you can find in your research about both musicians. Then make a single statement about each musician that reflects the main idea of the information you found about them. (Technology)

4. Listen to a rap song (a clean one!) and memorize its lyrics. Present the rap song for your class. (Speaking/Listening)

NEWSPAPER COLUMNS

"I WAS AN APPALOOSA, IN SEARCH OF HALLOWEEN LOOT"
(by Craig Wilson, *USA Today*)
"A GIFT TO REMEMBER" (by Ellen Goodman, *The Boston Globe*)

Learning Strategy:	Summarizing
Reading Skill:	Comparing and Contrasting
Test-Taking Strategy:	Personal Response Essay

Setting the Scene

Every newspaper has columnists who serve as a voice, a conscience, a commentator for its readers. Some columnists, like Craig Wilson and Ellen Goodman, reach national fame for their humor or their succinct analysis of popular culture or politics. Both of these columnists are award-winners; clearly they have a following who appreciates their work.

Begin this lesson by bringing a copy of your own local paper to class and inviting students to read aloud one of the regular columnists—you may even have Ellen Goodman carried in your paper via syndication. Or, you might bring in a Wednesday copy of USA Today and find Craig Wilson's column "The Final Word" in the Life section. Engage students in a discussion of why newspapers use columnists on their op-ed pages and what role these columnists play in the day-to-day life of newspaper readers.

Ask students to discuss the importance of newspaper columnists in all their various styles. What role do they feel these writers play for their readers? Why do they think that readers return to columnists' work time and time again?

Introducing the Skill

Use a non-text example to begin the lesson on comparing and contrasting. Ask students to compare and contrast two different objects in the classroom, such as two different plants, pictures, books, posters, artwork. Ask the class to discuss ways these objects are alike and ways they are different. Be sure to choose objects that are ordinary and used every day. Emphasize how often they can use the skill of comparing and contrasting. Show students how to apply this skill in other subject areas as well, such as social studies/history, English literature, sports, or even math.

Especially for English Language Learners

Sharing Culture Halloween is a phenomenon that is not shared by all cultures. You may want to explain to your ELLs the ritual of Halloween and why people dress up and go door-to-door looking for treats. Invite those for whom Halloween is a regular tradition to talk about some experiences they have had that might even be similar to the one Craig Wilson describes in his column. Allow your ELLs to express their views of Halloween. For many, All Saints' Day may have a significantly different meaning and for some people, Halloween may have a negative or even offensive connotation. Be sure to keep the discussion open so that everyone can express his or her point of view.

Sharing Language Craig Wilson uses many slang idioms in his column piece on being an appaloosa on Halloween. Before you read, go over these expressions and ask your ELLs to guess at what the meanings might be. Then ask your native speakers to try to explain these idioms—and better yet, where they come from. Here are a few that might cause some problems:

loot	shenanigans
pickings were slim	vaudeville act
rabble-rousers	mayhem

Assessing Understanding

Personal response is not as widely used on standardized tests as it is in the classroom and within school districts. However, it is a very useful tool, particularly for use in portfolio assessments used within school buildings and districts. Portfolios offer a very personalized look at the growth of any individual student throughout the year.

A personal response statement can show several things: First, it can reflect a student's understanding of the text as she or he interacts with it. A student can identify with the events, characters, or ideas they are reading about and help themselves to focus even more on their own ideas or beliefs. Second, a personal response is an opportunity to see how a student organizes written information in an informal way. This helps to determine how many writing skills come easily to the student. Third, a personal response enables you to see if there are any areas in which an individual student needs help or remediation.

It is useful to use a variety of assessments throughout the school year, including portfolios containing personal responses. Working with you, students can assess their own growth throughout the year and can take part in their own assessment. This helps them as they set goals for the coming semesters and years.

Reading Further

I Know Just What You Mean . . . The Power of Friendship in Women's Lives by Patricia O'Brien and Ellen Goodman, Simon & Schuster: New York.

Extending to Technology

To find more information on-line, use the following search terms: Ellen Goodman and Craig Wilson. Or visit these web sites:

Ellen Goodman quotations:
www.womenshistory.miningco.com/library/qu/blqugood.htm
www.bemorecreative.com

Interview with Washington Press Club:
www.npc.press.org/wpforal/good1.htm

Craig Wilson columns:
www.USAToday.com

Ellen Goodman columns:
www.BostonGlobe.com

NEWSPAPER COLUMNS

"I WAS AN APPALOOSA, IN SEARCH OF HALLOWEEN LOOT"
(by Craig Wilson, *USA Today*)
"A GIFT TO REMEMBER" (by Ellen Goodman, *The Boston Globe*)

Learning Strategy:	Summarizing
Reading Skill:	Comparing and Contrasting
Test-Taking Strategy:	Personal Response Essay

STEP 1: LINK IT

Before You Read

Who among your friends is a great storyteller? What makes your friend's stories so great? Are they funny? Are they suspenseful? Does your friend use a lot of vivid detail to show what happened? Can you often relate to what happened to your friend almost as if it happened to you?

Good storytellers can tell a story and make you feel what they feel. Good storytellers are great to listen to—they can make you laugh, cry, and especially think. The best storytellers can carve meaning from very simple moments and apply that meaning to life in general.

People can tell great stories orally and in writing. You are about to read two stories written by newspaper columnists Craig Wilson and Ellen Goodman. These two writers contribute regularly to newspapers read by thousands of people. Wilson's writing often evokes a mood, making the reader remember, think, or laugh out loud. Goodman's columns tend to be more political in nature, using everyday events to provoke a way of thinking about the world. Both writers are great storytellers.

As you read, think about how each writer tells his or her story. Read closely and think about what part makes you laugh, what part makes you sad (if any), what part makes you think, and most important, what part you feel you can identify with. On the lines on the next page, make a list of four or five things you think make a good story. Then check back after you have finished reading.

A good story has:

1. _____

2. _____

3. _____

4. _____

5. _____

Set a Strategy

You are going to be reading two articles by two different writers. You are going to have to understand what each article *says.* You will also need to know what each article *means.* This way you will be able to talk about them with confidence, especially as you compare them.

Earlier, you learned how to find the main idea by adding up all of the details and creating one sentence that told what the main point of the article on Maya Lin was all about. Now you are going to learn about another reading strategy that goes one step further than finding the main idea. This strategy is called **summarizing.**

Summarizing is a process of organizing what you read. First, you find the most important points, (or characters, or events). Then you find the most important details, and then you state these points briefly in your own words. This strategy is useful because it can help you remember what you read as well as help you monitor your own understanding. Summarizing can help you discover the information that is most important to the author. It can also help you better analyze what you read. If you cannot summarize what you have read, then you do not understand it. If you can, then you can build on what you've learned, and better understand what you read.

The three main characteristics of a summary:

• It is brief.

• It includes the main idea and the most important details.

• It is organized with the most important ideas first and the details second.

Work with a partner to read the two articles that follow. Choose one partner to read and the other to take notes for the first article. Switch roles for the second article. The reader should silently read the article first to get a sense of what it is about. Then the reader should read aloud while the listener takes notes. (See the end of the article for a place to take notes.) The listener should list the most important ideas and then add important details as he or she listens. After the reader has read the article once, the listener should write a summary of what he or she has heard. Then compare your summaries with those of the rest of the class. Remember to follow the three main characteristics for a summary.

Set a Purpose

The articles you are about to read are newspaper columns—short observations written from the author's viewpoint. Columns do not contain a lot of heavy factual information; rather they are lighter pieces you might read to give you a new look at something going on in the world. For this reason, you might not give a column the same type of close reading that you would an encyclopedia entry. It doesn't matter if you forget some of the facts of a column. It does matter that you understand the main point of what you read. Your main purpose in reading these articles is to see what the authors think about what they are writing about. Then you can decide if you agree or disagree, or if you have shared some of the same experiences as the writers.

STEP 2: READ IT

Craig Wilson is a regular columnist for USA Today *as well as a feature reporter. His "Final Word" is often a humorous glimpse of the author's life and reflections of life in general. Readers can often relate to him, since his experiences are often mirrored in theirs—especially as new generations change the "rules" of how things are done.*

"I Was an Appaloosa, in Search of Halloween Loot"

Growing up in the country has its advantages. Trick-or-treating is not one of them.

I remember how envious I was of the kids in town, the ones who had hundreds
5 of houses to go to. I had images of them running from porch to lighted porch, bags so filled with candy they had to be dragged along.

I grew up on a farm, but our place was on the edge of a hamlet of 10 houses, population 52. The place was so small we couldn't even be called a crossroads because the two roads we had didn't cross. They only made a T.

10 On Halloween, the pickings were slim. Auntie Bernice, over on the other road, gave out popcorn balls, which to an 8-year-old in the country seemed quite exotic. They were in plastic wrap, tied up with orange ribbon. The rest of the lot weren't so creative, offering nothing more original than M&Ms. One neighbor gave out dimes. One dime per kid. Yes, she was odd.

15 But whatever we got was never enough to even cover the bottom of the bag. We could have held all the Halloween candy we gathered in a small lunch bag, but having the optimism of youth, year after year, we lugged shopping bags. It didn't help matters any that two houses never gave out anything, their porch lights as dark as the owners' spirit.

20 The whole trick-or-treat journey could be done in less than 20 minutes. Then we'd return home, all dressed up with no place left to go.

In the meantime, the older kids, which included my brother and his gang of rabble-rousers, were out being creative—soaping windows and toilet-papering trees. They were 12. Far too cool to trick-or-treat.

25 One year, their Halloween shenanigans got the better of them when they over-turned Laverne Hall's outhouse and in their panic to escape found themselves falling into the hole. My biggest regret in life is I wasn't there to witness it. To

make matters better, they had to be hosed down before they could enter the house.

30   My pal Patty Miller often accompanied me on my Halloween rounds. She lived up the road and viewed our trick-or-treat situation as I did. Pathetic.

    So one year, we decided we would branch out. We would not be confined by the borders of our dreary little life. We would walk down roads not taken.

    I was an Appaloosa horse that year. Brown and white. My costume's mask was 35 so long that whenever I moved my head quickly, I bumped into things, like Patty Miller. The tail was so long, it needed to be held.

    Patty was a hobo, so when I wasn't bumping her with my horse head, she was hitting me with the hobo stick that rested on her shoulder. We were a vaudeville act, trapped in the farmlands of upstate New York.

40   Once we finished the 10 houses, we made our move. There were a couple of houses half a mile down the road. Untapped territory. We would go to them, get more candy and keep moving. Maybe we'd walk all the way into town, eight miles away.

    The fact that we both were terrified was never discussed. It didn't need to be. I 45 remember cars barreling down the highway toward us. We must have been a sight. A hobo clutching an Appaloosa clutching his own tail. But no one stopped. No one even slowed down.

    When we approached one of the houses we'd never been to before, we saw the porch light was on. Our hearts raced. Then, all of a sudden, out of the sky, maybe 50 a tree, fell two bodies. They could have been ghosts.

    What followed was panic, chaos and mayhem.

    I wet my Appaloosa horse costume right there on the spot. And Patty Miller? She screamed a scream so long and so loud that I could believe it was still going on, except for the fact I saw her last year and she appears to have finally pulled 55 herself together.

    My brother, however, is *still* laughing.

Check Your Strategy

Notes for summarizing:

Main character(s): _____

_____

Main events: _____

_____

_____

_____

Key details: _____

_____

_____

_____

Summary: _____

_____

_____

_____

_____

_____

_____

_____

_____

_____

Ellen Goodman is a syndicated columnist for The Boston Globe. *She is also the author of several books and has won the coveted Pulitzer Prize for journalism. Her columns often join a personal experience with a more political, or global, objective look at the meaning of life's simpler moments.*

"A Gift to Remember"

The man stood in the checkout line, holding onto the new bicycle as if it were a prize horse. From time to time, he caressed the blue machine gently, stroking the handlebars, patting the seat, running his fingers across the red reflectors on
5 the pedals.

His pleasure, his delight, finally infected me. "It's a beautiful bike," I said to him, shifting my own bundles.

The man looked up sheepishly and explained. "It's for my son." Then he paused and, because I was a stranger, added, "I always wanted a bike like this
10 when I was a kid."

"Yes," I smiled. "I'm sure he'll love it."

The man continued absentmindedly handling his bicycle, and I looked around me in the Christmas line.

There were carts and carts full of presents. I wondered what was really in
15 them. How many others were buying gifts they always wished for. How many of us always give what we want, or wanted, to receive?

I've done it myself, I know that. Consciously or not. I've made up for the small longings, the silly disappointments of my own childhood, with my daughter's. The doll with long, long hair, the dog, the wooden dollhouse—these were all
20 absent from the holidays past.

I never told my parents when they missed the mark. How many of us did? I remember, sheepishly, the tin dollhouse, the parakeet, the doll with the "wrong" kind of hair.

Like most children, I was guilty about selfishness, about disappointment. I
25 didn't know what gap might exist between what my parents wanted to give and what they could give . . . but I thought about it.

I knew they cared and, so, even when it wasn't exactly right, I wanted to return something for my gift. I wanted to please my parents with my pleasure.

But standing in that line, I thought about what else is passed between people.
30 Gifts that come from a warehouse of feelings rather than goods.

Maybe we assume other people want what we want, and try to deliver it. Maybe in every season, we project from our needs, we giftwrap what was lacking in our own lives.

My parents, descendants of two volatile households, wanted to give us peace.
35 They did. But I am conscious now of also giving my child the right to be angry. In the same way, I know parents who came from rigid households and busily provide now what they needed then: freedom. They don't always feel their children's ache for "structure."

I know others who grew up in poor households and now make money as a life-
40 offering for their families. They don't understand when it isn't valued.

There are women so full of angry memories of childhood responsibilities that they can't comprehend their children's wish to help. There are men so busy making up for their fathers' disinterest that they can't recognize their sons' plea: lay off.

45 Every generation finds it hard sometimes to hear what our children need, to feel what they are missing, because our own childhood is still ringing in our ears.

It isn't just parents and children who miss this connection between giving and receiving. Husbands and wives, men and women, may also give what they want to get—caretaking, security, attention—and remain unsatisfied. Our most highly
50 prized sacrifices may lie unused under family trees.

Of course there are people who truly "exchange." The lucky ones are in fine tune. The careful ones listen to each other. They trade lists. They learn to separate the "me" from the "you." They stop rubbing balm on other people to relieve their own sore spots.

55 Perhaps the man in line with me is lucky or careful. I saw him wheel his gift through the front door humming, smiling. For a moment, I wondered if his son hinted for a basketball or a book. This time, I hope he wanted what his father wanted for him.

Check Your Strategy

Notes for summarizing:

Main character(s): _____

_____

Main events: _____

_____

_____

_____

Key details: _____

_____

_____

_____

Summary: _____

_____

_____

_____

_____

_____

_____

_____

_____

STEP 3: ASSESS IT

Check Your Understanding

Answer the following questions to be sure that you understand what you have read.

1. Why did Craig Wilson and his pal Patty Miller decide to venture farther than the borders of their usual trick-or-treating neighborhood?

   _____

   _____

2. In what way did Wilson's brother look at Halloween differently from Craig? Give evidence to support your point of view.

   _____

   _____

3. What do you think happened that made Craig "wet (his) Appaloosa horse costume" and Patty "scream a scream so long and so loud"?

   _____

   _____

4. What kind of a relationship do you think Craig had with his brother when they were young? What evidence can you find to support your thoughts?

   _____

   _____

5. Why did Ellen Goodman feel like talking to the man with the bicycle?

   _____

   _____

6. How did Goodman feel about some of her presents as a child?

_____

_____

7. What does Goodman mean when she says, "Maybe in every season, we project from our needs, we giftwrap what was lacking in our own lives"?

_____

_____

8. In one short sentence, Goodman says what she thinks the "careful" people should do to truly give to each other. What does she say? And what do you think she means by it?

_____

_____

Test-Taking Strategy

Some assessments ask you to respond to what you have read by writing a journal entry that shows how you relate to what the author has said. This type of assessment helps you determine if you understood the reading.

Read the following two questions. Then take 20 minutes to write your personal response to one of the questions. Remember to support your answers with specific reasons. If you run out of space, continue your answer on the back of the page. (For example, imagine that the question is *Why did you like the article by Craig Wilson?* You might answer, *Because it was funny.* Be sure to tell *why* you thought it was funny; for example, *I could remember what it was like to be eight years old and really serious about trick-or-treating, so I could relate to Craig's feelings. I could also as an older person, now, relate to his brother and why he thought it was funny to scare his little brother. And I could just picture those kids' faces when they got scared—it must have been quite a moment!*)

1. Why do you think Ellen Goodman's column is entitled "A Gift to Remember"? What gift is she talking about? What does she think needs to be remembered? What gift do you think should be remembered every holiday season?

   _____

   _____

   _____

   _____

   _____

   _____

   _____

2. Did Craig Wilson's column make you think of an experience when you were really scared but then everything turned out okay? What was that experience and how did you deal with it?

   _____

   _____

   _____

   _____

   _____

   _____

   _____

STEP 4: THINK ABOUT IT

You've just read two very different stories by newspaper columnists. These two people have the same job, yet they do their job in very different ways.

When you read two articles or stories that are of the same genre—such as a column—a helpful way to distinguish between them is by using a reading strategy called **comparing and contrasting.** When you **compare** two things, you analyze how they are alike. When you **contrast** two things, you analyze how they are different. For example, let's say you are asked to compare the two games of baseball and football. Here's how you might analyze these games using comparing and contrasting:

> *When I compare baseball and football, I discover there are many things in common. First of all, they are both played with a ball. Second, they both have two teams who play against one another, and the team with the highest score at the end wins the game. They are both mostly played outside. Both games have professional teams who are extremely well-paid for their participation. Both games play through a season and then vie for a major tournament at the end of the season. Both games have players who are traded among teams. Both games require a lot of running. Both games have team coaches.*

You could come up with even more ways the games are alike. If you were to contrast the two games, this might be something like what you would discover:

> *When I contrast baseball and football, I find that they have a lot of differences. The ball in baseball is small and round and fits in a player's hand. In football, the ball is made of pigskin and it is oval. In football, players throw the ball and kick the ball. In baseball, they bat the ball. In football, teams score goals; in baseball, they score runs. Football games are divided into quarters; baseball games are divided into innings. The football field is rectangular and is divided into yards. The baseball field is diamond-shaped and is divided into bases. In football, players wear shoulder pads; in baseball, players do not.* Again, there are many other differences, but you can fill them in from here!

Comparing and Contrasting

When you read, you use comparing and contrasting to analyze the similarities and differences among characters, events, facts, or authors. You use comparing and contrasting when you are reading for information (for example, to compare and contrast facts), and when you are reading a story (for example, to compare and contrast characters). You can use this strategy any time you read. Knowing how to compare and contrast can help you organize what you've read and then analyze it.

On the lines below, brainstorm at least three ways the articles by Wilson and Goodman are alike. Then brainstorm how they are different.

How they are alike (compare):

1. Example: *They are both written by newspaper columnists.*

2. _____

3. _____

4. _____

5. _____

How they are different (contrast):

1. Example: *The Wilson article makes me laugh; the Goodman article makes me think.*

2. _____

3. _____

4. _____

5. _____

Look at It Another Way

Another way to look at comparing and contrasting is to create a graphic organizer called a Venn diagram. A Venn diagram is two circles that overlap in the middle. The two circles represent the things being compared. The overlap shows where these two things have similarities. The part that doesn't overlap illustrates where the two things are different.

Look at the Venn diagram below. Fill in your examples of how the articles are alike and different. Use the Venn diagram any time you are comparing and contrasting two things—it makes a quick and easy visual.

"I Was an Appaloosa in Search of Halloween Loot"   "A Gift to Remember"

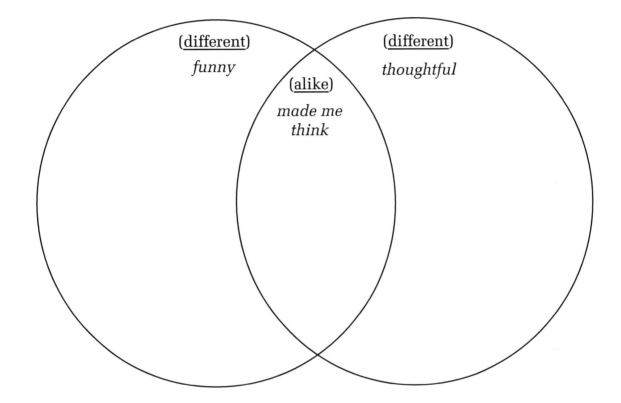

STEP 5: RELATE IT

1. Take a look at your local newspaper and identify the regular columnists. Who are they and what type of column do they write? Are
   there any that you particularly like or agree with? Read three or four
   columns by one of your favorite columnists. Then summarize each
   of the columns and present your summary to the class orally. (Speaking/
   Listening)

2. Log on to USAToday.com and find several of Craig Wilson's
   columns. (They are part of the Life Section called "The Final
   Word.") Read some of the columns and then create a chart that
   compares and contrasts them. What are the common threads that
   run through his columns? How are these columns different? (Technology)

3. Using charcoal or pencil, choose a moment from either Craig
   Wilson's or Ellen Goodman's column and illustrate it. Use the
   details the writer gives to determine details. You may need to fill in
   any details you don't know using your own artistic license. (Visual)

4. Imagine you have been asked to write the teleplay (a script for television) for either Craig Wilson's or Ellen Goodman's column. Turn
   the column into a script, complete with stage directions and specific
   dialogue for each character. Write your teleplay and then, if there's
   time, invite your classmates to perform it. (Writing)

SPEECH

"I HAVE A DREAM"
(by Martin Luther King, Jr.)

Learning Strategy:	Recognizing Setting
Reading Skill:	Understanding Use of Literary Devices
Test-Taking Strategy:	Recall/Comprehension

Setting the Scene

"I Have a Dream" is only one of Martin Luther King's impassioned speeches that became the cornerstone of the Civil Rights movement of the 1950s and 1960s. Because of his extraordinary ability to touch, inspire, and ultimately move, the lives of all Americans were forever changed. He was able to give a voice to those who had previously been silent, and he embodied extreme courage in his quest for equality of the races. Most of your students will know Dr. King—they are used to a holiday in January to celebrate his birthday, and undoubtedly they studied his life in elementary school. Students will surely know that Dr. King was killed before he turned forty by an assassin in April 1968. Now, as they examine this speech and look at Dr. King's words anew, students may want to think about the sacrifices that this man made for what he considered a "greater" good. You may want to discuss with your students what issues they would be willing to stand up for, what causes matter to them, what "greater good" they would fight for.

Introducing the Skill

The best way to appreciate Dr. King's speech is to hear it. If you can, find a recording of the actual 1963 speech. (A recording can be found in *Great Speeches of the Twentieth Century.*) If it is hard to obtain a recording, read it aloud or propose that your students take turns reading it aloud. By listening to the speech, learners can focus on the way it changes from the beginning to the end. In the beginning, listeners may be able to tell that Dr. King might have been nervous and possibly distracted by the noises from airplanes, traffic, or the crowd. As the speech goes on, he gets more and more confident, as you can hear by the resonance of his words and strength of his voice. Elicit students' reactions to the way the speech is given.

You may want to explain to learners that they will be hearing a speech that makes use of beautiful literary devices. As students approach the lesson skill, remind them that when they recognize these devices—such as repetition, assonance, or imagery—they will come to appreciate what they are listening to—or reading— much more. Encourage them to listen for these devices when they read, when they listen to a speaker, or even when listening to the radio or television. Elicit from them that they may feel that a speech is "better" because of the use of these devices.

Teacher Guide

Especially for English Language Learners

Sharing Culture Invite students to tell what they may know already about Martin Luther King, Jr. Ask them if they have studied him in school, and if so, what message they were taught about him. Then invite them to discuss great speakers and leaders from their country of origin. Have they heard a great speech? Who gave it? What was it about? Perhaps they heard a great speech that had a message in it they did *not* like, but which inspired people nonetheless. What were the things that made that speech memorable? How did the speaker use words to set a tone, to inspire, to move his or her audience?

Sharing Language In his speech, Dr. King refers to "the Negro." Remind learners that this is a word that was used to describe those who were of African ancestry. Many of the "Negroes" who were in the crowd that day in August 1963 were descended from slaves who were brought to the United States against their will during the eighteenth and nineteenth centuries. Explain that the term "Negro" is no longer used to describe people of African descent. In the 1960s through the 1990s, and still widely accepted, is the word "black" to describe those of African heritage. Today, most people use the word "African American" to describe those of African heritage.

Assessing Understanding

In the **Assess It** section of the student lesson on page 71, learners use their critical-thinking skills to first recall, then synthesize and evaluate their responses to Dr. King's speech. They will also work together to create a "test prep" to reflect standardized vocabulary comprehension found on state tests. If you are able to retrieve a sample of your state's assessment

tests—such as the TAAS (Texas Assessment of Academic Skills 1999), Ohio Proficiency Test (1995), Virginia Literacy Passport Program (1994), or CAPT (Connecticut Academic Performance Test 1995), you may want to create samples based on their multiple-choice format to test your students so that they become completely familiar with the state testing formats.

Reading Further

There are many, many volumes written about Dr. King. Students will find whole library shelves devoted to him, to his speeches, and to his times. However, the work of Martin Luther King, Jr., is best outlined in his own words, which were always eloquent and inspiring.

I Have a Dream: Writings and Speeches that Change the World, James Melvin Washington (editor), Martin Luther King, Jr., HarperSan Francisco.

The Autobiography of Martin Luther King, Jr., Clayborne Carson (editor), Martin Luther King, Jr., Warner Books.

A Testament of Hope: The Essential Writings of Martin Luther King, Jr., James Melvin Washington (editor), HarperCollins.

Taylor Branch won the Pulitzer Prize for his book *Parting the Waters: America in the King Years 1953–1963* (Simon & Schuster). The companion to this book is *Pillar of Fire: America in the King Years 1963–1965* (Simon & Schuster).

Extending to Technology

To find more information on-line, use the following search terms: Martin Luther King, Jr., Civil Rights movement, and Nobel Peace Prize. Or visit these web sites:
mlkonline.com
martinlutherking.8m.com
SeattleTimes.com

SPEECH

5

"I HAVE A DREAM"
by Martin Luther King, Jr.

Learning Strategy:	Recognizing Setting
Reading Skill:	Understanding Use of Literary Devices
Test-Taking Strategy:	Recall/Comprehension

STEP 1: LINK IT

Before You Read

On a steamy summer's day in late August 1963, more that 200,000 people gathered in Washington, D.C. They were there to march for equal rights for all Americans. The pivotal event of the day was a speech made by the eloquent Reverend Martin Luther King, Jr.

It was during his college and graduate school studies that Dr. King was most profoundly influenced by Mohandas Ghandi, an Indian leader who believed in the idea of social change through nonviolent demonstration. Dr. King was offered numerous positions as a college professor—a job that would have been fairly easy for him. However, King knew that he was meant to be a preacher, so he accepted a post as pastor of the Dexter Baptist Church in Montgomery, Alabama. It was there that King became involved with the boycott of the Montgomery bus system after Rosa Parks refused to follow the law and sit at the back of the bus. From there, King rose to national prominence, mostly because he had a gift of speech. That speech would inspire, motivate, and resonate with hundreds of thousands of people from all over the country.

It was his "I Have a Dream" speech that really marked the peak of King's career. This was the speech that brought the fight for equality to the attention of the entire nation.

Think of speeches that you have heard live. What about them have you liked? What about them have you disliked? Have you ever heard a speech that inspired you? What was it the speaker did that moved you? What qualities do you think are most necessary to be a great speaker?

Set a Strategy

Dr. King gave his speech in front of the Lincoln Memorial in Washington, D.C. As he spoke, airplanes thundered overhead. People in the audience shouted, clapped, and cheered along with him as he spoke. What do you think Dr. King saw, heard, and felt as he began his speech? As you read, think about how the setting of the speech might contribute to the way Dr. King delivered his speech. Think, too, about how the setting might add even more meaning to the words Dr. King spoke. Take a minute to list some of the things about the setting that might make the speech even more meaningful.

_____

_____

_____

_____

Set a Purpose

Have you ever heard a really good speech? What was good about it? Was it the message? Was it the content? Or was it the *way* the person delivered the speech? Studies have shown that after a few days, people remember only two percent of what they hear in a speech. What they do remember is *how* the speech was delivered. They remember the speaker's enthusiasm. They remember whether the speech was uplifting or somber. They remember if they felt moved or inspired. These things—the things you and many others remember in a speech—are what make up the *tone* of the speech.

In many speeches, the tone is set by the way the speaker uses words to convey his or her message. By using various literary techniques, the speaker can inspire emotion and move the audience to action. As you read Dr. King's speech, look for the way he uses language to set a tone. For example, does he repeat words or phrases? Does he try to paint a picture with words? Finally, think about what message Dr. King was hoping his audience would remember days, months, or even years later.

STEP 2: READ IT

Dr. King and the 200,000 white and black people who joined him in August 1963 made history. Never before had so many people congregated for any cause. Specifically, they gathered to persuade Congress to pass a bill that would guarantee equal rights. The march was a success. In 1964, Congress passed the Civil Rights Bill. Also in 1964, Martin Luther King, Jr., was awarded the highest honor in the world: the Nobel Peace Prize. Many historians would agree that this speech is the greatest of the twentieth century. As you read, determine what you think made it so great a speech.

Five score years ago, a great American, in whose symbolic shadow we stand, signed the Emancipation Proclamation. This momentous decree came as a great beacon light of hope to millions of Negro slaves who had been seared in the flames of withering injustice. It came as a joyous daybreak to end the long night

5 of captivity.

But one hundred years later, we must face the tragic fact that the Negro is still not free. One hundred years later, the life of the Negro is still sadly crippled by the manacles of segregation and the chains of discrimination. One hundred years later, the Negro lives on a lonely island of poverty in the midst of a vast ocean of

10 material prosperity. One hundred years later, the Negro is still languishing in the corners of American society and finds himself an exile in his own land. So we have come here today to dramatize an appalling condition.

In a sense we have come to our nation's capital to cash a check. When the architects of our republic wrote the magnificent words of the Constitution and

15 the Declaration of Independence, they were signing a promissory note to which every American was to fall heir. This note was a promise that all men—yes, black men as well as white men—would be guaranteed the unalienable rights of life, liberty, and the pursuit of happiness.

It is obvious today that America has defaulted on this promissory note insofar

20 as her citizens of color are concerned. Instead of honoring this sacred obligation, America has given the Negro people a bad check, a check which has come back marked "insufficient funds." But we refuse to believe that there are insufficient funds in the great vaults of opportunity of this nation. So we have come to cash this check—a check that will give us upon demand the riches of freedom and the

25 security of justice. We have also come to this hallowed spot to remind America of the fierce urgency of *now.* This is no time to engage in the luxury of cooling off or to take the tranquilizing drugs of gradualism. *Now* is the time to make real the promises of Democracy. . . . *Now* is the time to open the doors of opportunity to all of God's children. *Now* is the time to lift our nation from the quicksands of 30 racial injustice to the solid rock of brotherhood . . .

    . . . And as we walk, we must make the pledge that we shall march ahead. We cannot turn back. There are those who are asking the devotees of civil rights, "When will you be satisfied?" We can never be satisfied as long as the Negro is the victim of the unspeakable horrors of police brutality. We can never be satis-35 fied as long as our bodies, heavy with the fatigue of travel, cannot gain lodging in the motels of the highways and hotels of the cities. We cannot be satisfied as long as the Negro's basic mobility is from a smaller ghetto to a larger one. We can never be satisfied as long as a Negro in Mississippi cannot vote and a Negro in New York believes he has nothing for which to vote. No, no, we are not satisfied, 40 and we will not be satisfied until justice rolls down like waters and righteousness like a mighty stream.

    I am not unmindful that some of you have come here out of great trials and tribulations. Some of you have come fresh from narrow jail cells. Some of you have come from areas where your quest for freedom left you battered by the 45 storms of persecution and staggered by the winds of police brutality. You have been the veterans of creative suffering. Continue to work with the faith that unearned suffering is redemptive.

    Go back to Mississippi, go back to Alabama, go back to South Carolina, go back to Georgia, go back to Louisiana, go back to the slums and ghettos of our northern 50 cities, knowing that somehow this situation can and will be changed. Let us not wallow in the valley of despair.

    I say to you today, my friends, that in spite of the difficulties and frustrations of the moment I still have a dream. It is a dream deeply rooted in the American dream.

55   I have a dream that one day this nation will rise up and live out the true meaning of its creed: "We hold these truths to be self-evident, that all men are created equal."

I have a dream that one day on the red hills of Georgia the sons of former slaves and the sons of former slaveowners will be able to sit down together at the table
60 of brotherhood.

I have a dream that one day even the state of Mississippi, a desert state sweltering with the heat of injustice and oppression, will be transformed into an oasis of freedom and justice.

I have a dream that my four little children will one day live in a nation where
65 they will not be judged by the color of their skin but by the content of their character.

I have a dream today.

I have a dream that one day the state of Alabama, whose governor's lips are presently dripping with the words of interposition and nullification, will be
70 transformed into a situation where little black boys and black girls will be able to join hands with little white boys and white girls and walk together as sisters and brothers.

I have a dream today.

I have a dream that one day every valley shall be exalted, every hill and moun-
75 tain shall be made low, the rough places will be made plain, and the crooked places will be made straight, and the glory of the Lord shall be revealed, and all flesh shall see it together.

This is our hope. This is the faith with which I return to the South. With this faith we will be able to hew out of the mountain of despair a stone of hope. With
80 this faith we will be able to transform the jangling discords of our nations into a beautiful symphony of brotherhood. With this faith we will be able to work together, to pray together, to struggle together, to go to jail together, to stand up for freedom together, knowing that we will be free one day.

This will be the day when all of God's children will be able to sing with new
85 meaning

My country 'tis of thee,
Sweet land of liberty,
Of thee I sing:

90 　　　　　Land where my fathers died,
　　　　　Land of the pilgrims' pride,
　　　　　From every mountainside,
　　　　　　Let freedom ring.
　　So let freedom ring from the prodigious hilltops of New Hampshire. Let free-
dom ring from the mighty mountains of New York. Let freedom ring from the
95 heightening Alleghenies of Pennsylvania. Let freedom ring from the snowcapped
Rockies of Colorado. Let freedom ring from the curvaceous peaks of California.
　　But not only that. Let freedom ring from Stone Mountain of Georgia. Let freedom ring from Lookout Mountain of Tennessee. Let freedom ring from every hill
and molehill of Mississippi. From every mountainside, let freedom ring.
100 　　When we let freedom ring, when we let it ring from every village and every
hamlet, from every state and every city, we will be able to speed up that day
when all of God's children, black men and white men, Jews and Gentiles, Protes-
tants and Catholics, will be able to join hands and sing in the words of the old
Negro spiritual, "Free at last! Free at last! Thank God almighty, we are free at
105 last!"

STEP 3: ASSESS IT
React
What is your immediate reaction to this speech? Does it move you? Are you inspired at all? Or are there parts of it that you feel are better than others? Write your reactions to the speech. Is there any part of it that you identify with? What words might you use to describe this speech? Dull? Impassioned? Repetitious? Inspired? Continue your answers on the back of the page.

_____

_____

_____

Check Your Understanding
Read the following questions and write a sentence to answer each.

1. What message do you think Dr. King was hoping people would get from his speech?

_____

_____

2. Often a speaker will use specific techniques to make the speech more memorable. In this speech, Dr. King repeats key phrases. What are some examples of repetition in this speech?

_____

_____

3. What are some visual images Dr. King uses to paint a picture and therefore help his audience understand his message?

_____

_____

4. Dr. King often uses quotations from other sources in his speeches to illustrate his points. Do you recognize any quotations? If not, are there some you might guess are from other places?

_____

_____

Test-Taking Strategy

In many standardized tests, you will be asked to recall key points from what you have read. In these instances, you will be given a question and then multiple answers from which to choose the best response. This type of test is called a multiple choice. No doubt you have taken multiple-choice tests before.

Multiple-choice tests are often used to test your recall and your understanding—or comprehension—of what you have read. Sometimes you will be able to go back to the text to answer your questions. Other times, you won't, and you will be asked to remember the key points. This is a time to really use your main idea and detail strategies. Before you take a multiple-choice test based on an excerpt or reading, be sure that you know what the main idea and supporting details are. Chances are, you will then be able to answer most of the multiple-choice questions. When answering a multiple-choice question, be sure to eliminate the answers you know are incorrect. Then use your best recall or comprehension to answer the questions.

Now try your hand at creating a multiple-choice test for a partner or small group in your class. Try not to focus on specific or small details; rather, focus on key points. Then, when you create the four responses (usually there are four: a, b, c, and d), make sure that at least two of the answers are possibilities. Here are two examples:

1. *What does Dr. King mean when he says, "In a sense we have come to our nation's capital to cash a check."*

    a. *The Constitution promised that all men would have equal rights, but up to this point, black people had not been able to "make good" on that promise.*

    b. *The Constitution said specifically that "all black men and women have the same rights as white men and women," and Dr. King wanted to be sure that everyone knew this.*

   c. *President Lincoln had promised that all black people would be given a certain amount of money.*

   d. *Dr. King was hoping that everyone at the gathering in Washington would go to the bank and give him money.*

  2. *Dr. King says that people ask him when black people will be satisfied. He tells them:*

   a. *They will be satisfied when every one of them has a great job.*

   b. *They will be satisfied when every "Negro" can own a car.*

   c. *They will be satisfied when every black person can stay in any hotel, live anywhere, vote, and experience the true meaning of justice.*

   d. *They will be satisfied when the Constitution is rewritten by a black person.*

STEP 4: THINK ABOUT IT

Dr. King felt that "a leader has to be concerned with semantics." He meant that great leaders need to know how to speak clearly and in a way that inspires others. Dr. King had plenty of practice as the son of a Baptist minister, and as a Baptist minister himself. Growing up in the church as he did, he had many opportunities to speak aloud, as this type of oratory is a large part of the church.

Literary Devices

But Dr. King went further than most people who speak in public. He was a gifted storyteller. And he also used a number of **literary devices** to color his speeches. A literary device is a technique that forms a visual image or sound to enhance the message of the story, article, or speech.

Imagery

Dr. King used several literary devices in his speeches. One important device is called **imagery.** Imagery is the use of descriptive words and phrases to create vivid pictures for the reader or listener. When Dr. King talks about the sons of slaves and the sons of slaveowners being able to sit down at the "table of brotherhood," he conjures a visual image for the listener of a real table where you can picture black people and white people sitting together. Dr. King could have just as easily said, "It will be great when one day black people and white people talk to each other." This would not have had the same impact as the idea of these people with dissimilar backgrounds (the children of slaves and the children of slaveowners) sitting at a table together.

Simile

Another device Dr. King uses is **simile.** A simile is a statement that compares one thing to another using *like* or *as.* Here are some examples of Dr. King's use of similes:

"This momentous decree came **as** a great beacon light of hope . . ."

"It came **as** a joyous daybreak to end the long night of captivity . . ."

Can you find another simile? Write it below.

_____

_____

Metaphor

Dr. King also uses a device called **metaphor.** Metaphor is like simile except that it doesn't use *like* or *as* in its comparison. There are many metaphors in Dr. King's speech. Here are several examples from just one paragraph:

". . . the life of the Negro is still sadly **crippled by the manacles of segregation** and the **chains of discrimination.** One hundred years later, **the Negro lives on a lonely island** of poverty in the midst of a **vast ocean of material prosperity.** One hundred years later, **the Negro is still languishing in the corners** of American society and finds himself an exile in his own land."

In analyzing this passage, you know from your own prior knowledge that the "Negro," meaning all Negroes, was not physically "crippled" by anything. But Dr. King uses a metaphor as he compares a whole group of people to just one person who is "crippled." He then says that the "Negro lives on a lonely island . . . " Again, he is suggesting that all African Americans are suffering the same physical fate of living on a lonely island. Are they? Is even one person living on that island? No, but it makes a great visual image and it invokes a feeling of desolation and loneliness for a whole group of people—just what Dr. King wants it to do.

What are some other metaphors in the speech? On the following lines, write at least three more metaphors you find. Then write what you think that metaphor was meant to illustrate.

1. metaphor: _____

   illustration: _____

2. metaphor: _____

   illustration: _____

3. metaphor: _____

   illustration: _____

Anaphora

Another literary device that Dr. King uses is called **anaphora.** Anaphora is the repeated use of words or phrases. In the "I Have a Dream" speech, Dr. King repeats the phrase "Let freedom ring" 11 times. He repeats "I have a dream" eight times. What do you think this technique does for a speech? Often it helps to focus the attention of the listener during the speech, in a sense giving the listener time to "catch up" with what is being said. It is a little like using a person's name when you talk to ensure that person is paying attention. Anaphora also lends an almost musical sound to a speech, making it very easy to listen to—rhythmic and soothing, like a gentle song.

Look at It Another Way

You can create a graphic device to help you remember the various literary techniques from Dr. King's speech. Look at the chart below. Write the meanings of each of the literary devices next to them. Find a **new** example from Dr. King's speech of each device and add it to the chart. Then create one of your own and write it in the last column.

Device	Definition	Example	Your Example

STEP 5: RELATE IT

1. Obtain a copy of Dr. King's speech either in audio or audiovideo form. Listen carefully to the speech. Note the literary devices he uses throughout the speech. How do you think these devices contribute to the overall speech? Do you think that they help to make this one of the most memorable speeches of the twentieth century? (Speaking/Listening)

2. People who master the art of public speaking master an important skill. Interview various friends and family members and ask them who they think are great communicators. Then analyze what these people have in common. Finally, do some research on public speaking and create a poster that lists the "10 most important things you need to do to become a great public speaker." (Visual)

3. Go on-line and gather two or three of Dr. King's speeches. Analyze the various literary devices he uses. (One great speech is his last, given on April 3, 1968.) Create a chart that shows what these speeches have in common. How are they different? (Technology)

4. Write a speech! What subject do you feel strongly about? What could you say or do to inspire others to see your point of view and to persuade them to listen to you? Use various literary devices to enhance your speech—but still keep it in a conversational style. This will be a challenge! When you are done, deliver your speech to the class. (Writing)

ADVERTISEMENT

6

"COMPUTEASE COMPUTER LESSONS"
"PINE NEEDLE JUICE CAPSULES WEIGHT-LOSS PROGRAM"

Learning Strategy:	Reading Between the Lines
Reading Skill:	Recognizing Fact, Nonfact, and Claim
Test-Taking Strategy:	Short Answer Evaluation

Setting the Scene

Bring in print ads from various sources including trade journals, tabloids, fashion magazines, soap opera magazines, music magazines, cooking magazines, and anything else you think might appeal to your students. Invite them to discuss which ads are the most appealing and why. Which ads would make them want to buy something? Which ads turn them off?

Invite your students to discuss what the ads they like have in common. Help them analyze the techniques advertisers use to lure them into buying their products. Encourage students to talk about the ads they hear on the radio or see on television as well.

Advertising is huge business in the United States. To advertise during the Superbowl for less than one full minute costs over a million dollars. Ask students why they think advertising is so expensive. Engage them in a discussion of what life would be like without advertising.

Introducing the Skill

You will be introducing students to recognizing fact and nonfact in advertising. As you go through the print ads that you bring to class, ask students to discuss the claims that they read and whether or not they

think they are true or not. What makes students think that certain claims are true? What makes students suspect that others are not? Explain to students that they will be learning how to discern between fact and nonfact.

Especially for English Language Learners

Sharing Culture Engage your ELLs in a discussion about the root of advertising: capitalism. Explain that capitalism is an economic way of life that inspires free competition among businesses. Invite ELLs to discuss their own impressions of capitalism and what they like and don't like about it. Many of your ELLs will have come from countries where capitalism and advertising are not as important as they are in the United States.

Sharing Language Many of your ELLs will have a great grasp of grammar, having learned it more recently than your native speakers. They may find the syntax and fragments of advertising very confusing, since they have learned how to write in complete sentences using correct grammar. Explain to all of your students that advertisers take many liberties with their writing for various purposes, including to make the

77

Teacher Guide

ad copy seem to be a conversation between the reader and the advertiser.

Assessing Understanding

Students will be asked to react to the advertisements they read and to apply their own knowledge to what they read. Advertisers are adept at appealing to people and presenting claims as facts. Help your students develop a critical questioning habit to help them decide what is true and what is not. As they begin to answer the short answer questions in **Step 3: Assess It,** have them analyze their own reactions to the advertising material. What parts of the ads are the most convincing to them? Which parts can they dismiss out of hand?

Be sure that your students use critical-thinking skills to flesh out their responses to the ads. Here are some critical questions:

What evidence can I find that proves the claim?

What information is missing from the claim?

What facts support the conclusion that the advertisers make?

How do I know that the people who endorse the product are real?

Reading Further

Olgilvy on Advertising, by David Olgilvy, Random House.

20 Ads that Shook the World: The Century's Most Groundbreaking Advertising and How it Changed Us All by James B. Twitchell, Crown.

Adcult USA, James B. Twitchell, Columbia University Press.

Webonomics: Nine Essential Principles for Growing Your Business on the World Wide Web, Evan I. Schwartz, Broadway Books.

Extending to Technology

To find more information on-line, use the following search terms: advertising and media advertising. Or visit this web site: 4Advertising.com (news and commentary on the advertising industry)

ADVERTISEMENT

6

Learning Strategy:	Reading Between the Lines
Reading Skill:	Recognizing Fact, Nonfact, and Claim
Test-Taking Strategy:	Short Answer Evaluation

STEP 1: LINK IT

Before You Read

How many times have you bought a product or service because an ad promised you something you really wanted? How many times have you been completely satisfied by what you bought? If you have ever been disappointed by what you bought, you certainly aren't alone. This happens to people all day, every day. Advertising is very big business in the United States.

Why do companies spend so much money on advertising? Because there are so many competing companies out there who want you to buy their product, they are willing to spend a great deal of their money to tempt you to buy their product or service. After all, if you don't buy it, then they wouldn't sell anything, and they would go out of business. Advertising is an essential part of their business.

So what do advertisers do to tempt you to buy their product? Mostly they tell or show you how much your life would improve if you buy their product. Cosmetic companies show you young and beautiful models wearing their makeup. These ads tempt you to buy makeup by suggesting you will look as beautiful as their models. Sporting goods ads show you young, strong, powerful men and women wearing their shoes, shirts, shorts, or equipment. These companies are hoping you will want to be like the people in the ads. Your job as a consumer, or person buying and using products and services, is to be careful not to fall into the trap of believing exactly everything the advertisements suggest to you. In this lesson, you will read two ads that claim their products can help you learn everything about the computer and lose weight fast, fast, fast. As you read the ads, think how they remind you of other ads or infomercials you have seen and how easy it is to be tempted to buy their product.

1. Think about ads that you like. What do they have in common?

   _____

   _____

2. What are some ads that you don't like? What do they have in common?

   _____

   _____

3. What words make you believe in a product? _____

   _____

   _____

Set a Strategy

Have you ever had a new haircut or a new piece of clothing and asked someone how they like it—only to have them respond, "Um, it's different," or "How unusual"? You can tell from their response that they may not like what they see. How can you tell? They don't come right out and tell you that they don't like it, yet they don't say they like it either. But you can tell because you know them and you know how they usually react to something they like, and this isn't it. So while they haven't really come out and said anything, you know what they are really thinking—they don't like it! You probably use this strategy—**reading between the lines**—all the time.

Reading between the lines means "reading" the whole message that someone gives you. It means evaluating what is said, as well as asking questions about what is **not** said.

When you read an ad, you need to read between the lines very carefully. This means that you need to evaluate what is being said and decide if the whole truth is being given. Advertisers love to tell you something in a way that makes it seem very truthful, when in fact, they are leaving out important information. For example, in the ad for a product that will help you lose weight, you'll read, "Thanks to its fat-eliminating virtues, it is actually believed to be the most natural fat eater of all time." Here is a way you might analyze this statement by reading between the lines:

I'm going to break this statement down into two parts: first : "Thanks to its fat-eliminating virtues . . ." I ask myself, what is a fat-eliminating virtue? I know that eliminate means "get rid of." I know a virtue is a good quality. So this ad is saying that the product has the power to eliminate fat. But eliminate fat from where? Inside my body? In a food itself? This isn't really clear to me. More important is the second part: "it is actually believed to be the most natural fat eater of all time." What does it mean "it is believed"? Who believes it? The company that makes the product? Experts? What experts? People who use the product? This statement has no meaning since it is not based in fact. If I read between the lines here, I can tell that this is a statement that just sounds good, but doesn't really mean anything based on any facts.

As you read the two ads that follow, look carefully for statements that do not tell the whole story. Read between the lines—look for what is said, but more importantly, look for what isn't said—to determine if the statements give the whole message and tell the truth.

Set a Purpose

Advertising is something that you read or see or hear practically every day. All ads are written by creative people who are hoping that you will buy their product. Many ads use some kind of appeal to get you to enjoy their ad and buy their product. Some use humor, others use sentiment, still others use the promise of money, prestige, or romance. Your job is to decide whether or not you really need or want what someone is selling and to see through all these mechanisms.

As you read, remember to ask yourself the two questions: **What kind of writing is this?** This is advertising. It is not serious writing, yet it can affect your behavior if you believe everything you read! **Why am I reading this?** In this case, you are reading this to better see how advertisers use their words to tempt you, lure you, and often, deceive you into buying what they have to sell.

Name:

STEP 2: READ IT

The two ads that follow are made-up. But they are modeled on ads that you might find in a magazine. These "ads" are informational and have several things in common: They offer "authoritative" information, "expert" testimony, and testimony of "customers." Both ads make claims about what their product can do. Will you believe them?

Now you can make your computer as easy to use as a light switch!

Does your computer sit in the corner collecting dust? Have you read the manual and you still can't turn it on?

Well, here's news you've been waiting to hear!

Computease Press—under the advice of expert webmasters John Doe and Lillian Public—has developed a unique new computer-training experience. *Now you don't even have to read the manual!*

Here's how it works . . .

The Computease Home Course assumes you have never even used a computer. Never turned it on. Never heard a word of computer lingo. Nothing!

Every step—from turning the computer on to turning it off—is explained in step-by-step, easy-to-understand, *plain* English.

Every step is logical. You simply can't make a mistake, no matter how hard you try!

Here's what you get: the complete Computease course printed in large type on legal-size paper. We even include a sturdy vinyl cover, in case you spill your coffee!

And each lesson is fully illustrated with simple line drawings even a child could understand. So you can *actually see* every step of the way!

It comes ready-to-use. And we're so confident you'll complete the program successfully, we *unconditionally guarantee your results or your money back!*

It will take you about three hours—start to finish.

You'll learn how to navigate every software system sold on the market today, including desktop publishing!

Here's just some of the things you'll be able to do in just three short hours!

- You'll be able to recognize and identify every part of your computer and you'll know exactly how everything functions.
- You'll travel the world instantly by navigating the "world wide web" and "the Internet."
- You'll find out how you can get new programs for your computer absolutely **FREE!**
- You'll discover how to get on the information highway in a matter of seconds.
- You'll learn how to create and send messages to people all over the world!
- You'll learn to pay bills, manage your business, even do taxes!
- You'll discover how to keep bugs out of your computer forever—absolutely **FREE!**

- You'll learn how to take and send picture-perfect photos with just the click of the mouse—**FREE!**
- You'll learn how to protect your computer from floods, lightning, and other acts of God.
- You'll learn a secret way to get **FREE** radio stations from all over the world *and* hook them up to your own stereo system so you can listen *even when your computer isn't turned on!*
- You'll discover how to surf the Internet **FREE!**
- You'll be able to create your own newsletters, posters, artwork **FREE!**
- You'll be able to *talk* to anyone in the *world*—**FREE**—for up to 15 minutes!
- And much, much more . . .

Here are some comments from a few of our customers:

". . . This course is just what I needed to get me off my couch and back into the land of the living!"   Sue S., Portland, ME

". . . This course is so much better than those endless manuals that come with the computer. I threw mine away as soon as I got your course—and I have no regrets!"   Alan S., Tulsa, OK

". . . I'm a great-grandma and now I'm surfing the 'Net with folks half my age. I feel like I got a new lease on life!"   Deb E., Cumberland, MN

". . . I never thought I'd figure out the computer. But your course gave me new hope."   Margery N., Quebec, CA

". . . I use it to shop, shop, shop and I'll never stop. Thanks, Computease, for showing me the way!"   Kate O., Dublin, IL

A D V E R T I S E M E N T

AND NOW...

A Quick Weight-Loss Plan for People Who Can't Be Bothered with Diets

Did you know that pine needle juice was once used as a miraculous weight-loss liquid that also gave people remarkable energy boosts? Thanks to its fat-eliminating virtues, it is actually believed to be the most natural fat eater of all time!

This recently rediscovered mysterious liquid weight-loss substance is now available as weight-loss capsules with incredible life-changing results!

A few words from our clients:

I wanted to lose about 18 pounds quickly. I was able to do it in only 5 days! These capsules are the best weight-loss product I have ever tried. —*Lisa F., Martha's Vineyard, MA*

I tried the capsules and never had an aftertaste. And . . . I continue to eat as I usually do. I lost 22 pounds in 10 days. Thank you very much. —*Holly M., Walch, NY*

Your capsules are the best. I'll never try another diet again! —*Sheila R., Russell, OR*

I've stopped working out now that I've gotten a hold of these capsules, and boy do I look great, if I do say so myself! Thanks Pine Needle Juice, who would have thought it? —*David S., Newman, TX*

"I've maintained my girlish figure even when people my age have started to sag!" —*Ann S., Weston, AR*

A Simple Yet Brilliant Idea

The secret to eliminating fat deposits is to "open up the door" of the fat cells and allow them to drain the fat right out of them. The fat is then redirected to the bloodstream. Once it reaches the bloodstream, it is carried to the kidneys and then eliminated easily, quickly, painlessly! All you have to do is take the capsule! What could be more natural?

This Is Truly a Miracle Whose Time Has Come

The all-natural ingredients in these new pine needle juice capsules can also play an important role in stopping the development of new fat cells. They actually reverse the weight-gain process by causing existing fat cells to open up and drain off ugly body fat. The drained fat is then transported to the muscles where it can be burned off. This makes it possible to virtually eliminate fat deposits all over your body in no time at all!

FREQUENTLY ASKED QUESTIONS:
How Do the Pine Needle Capsules Work?

The capsules work like an "anti-fat battalion." The pine needle juice capsules transmit orders to the fat cells and offer a lubricant to drain and send fat to the muscles through the bloodstream. The muscles then burn fat and calories. The fat then slides out of your body during the course of natural elimination!

How Am I Losing Weight?

The pine needle juice capsules help to release the fat deposits that have accumulated on specific body areas such as the stomach, hips, legs, and back. They can also prevent new fat from penetrating the cells by redirecting it to the muscles where it is burned off, thereby eliminating fat deposits.

Isn't Pine Needle Juice Toxic?

Certainly not. In fact, quite the opposite is true. Have you ever seen a fat squirrel or a fat bird? The natural ingredients in pine needle juice have been feeding them for centuries. It's all natural biology—no chemistry involved! And with the pine needle juice capsules, you can eat anything you want and the fat just drips away!

When properly distributed, an intake of 5,000 calories a day can actually help you to lose weight instead of gain it. Because the capsules gently eliminate the toxins and excess weight, each day you'll feel better, more energized, and lose weight.

Fat Deposits Disappear in Record Time

If you want to lose weight quickly, order the new **unflavored** weight-loss pine needle juice capsules now. **They cost less than a dollar a day and work better than anything you've ever tried. If you don't agree, just return the empty bottle and we'll cheerfully refund your purchase price—no questions asked.**

The Fine Print: This weight loss plan is not intended to treat, diagnose, cure, or prevent any disease. Statements have not been evaluated by the FDA. Individual results vary and can be more or less than results mentioned.

A D V E R T I S E M E N T

STEP 3: ASSESS IT

React

Even though these ads are made up, they are quite like ads you might read in a newspaper or magazine. They are not really too far-fetched! What is your reaction to the ads? Do you want to buy the products? Do you believe everything that was said? Write your reactions, questions, and thoughts on the lines below.

_____

_____

_____

_____

_____

_____

Check Your Understanding

Answer the following questions to be sure that you got the main idea of the ads.

1. How long will it take you to take the Computease course?
   a. three days   c. three hours
   b. one day   d. two hours

2. For whom is the Computease computer course designed?
   a. computer classroom   c. computer beginners
      teachers
   b. senior citizens   d. business people

3. How do Pine Tree Juice Capsules work?
   a. They kill fat cells.
   b. They take away your appetite.
   c. They inspire you to become more physically active.
   d. They lubricate your system and help the fat slide out.

4. What is one thing Pine Tree Juice Capsules **can't** help you do?
   a. lose weight quickly   c. decrease your appetite
   b. eat anything you want   d. eliminate toxins

Test-Taking Strategy

On many standardized tests, you will be asked to evaluate what you have read. When you evaluate something, you use your prior knowledge plus your best reading skills to make a decision or a judgment about what you have read.

Evaluation questions are in-depth questions that require you to think critically about what you have read and to make a judgment based on your reading and on your own understanding. Here are some evaluation questions about the ads you have just read. Read each question below and then write your best answer on the lines below it.

1. Computease promises that you will learn at least 13 different things to do on the computer in just 3 hours. Do you think it is possible to learn that much in so short a time? Why or why not?

   _____

   _____

   _____

   _____

2. The Pine Tree Juice Capsules claim to be able to help you lose fat in a very short time. Do you think that the ad has supported this claim? Why or why not?

   _____

   _____

   _____

   _____

3. What are four specific questions you would ask the president of Computease about his or her product?

_____

_____

_____

_____

_____

_____

_____

_____

4. What "facts" support the conclusion that Pine Tree Juice Capsules can melt away fat? Do you believe these "facts"?

_____

_____

_____

_____

_____

_____

_____

_____

STEP 4: THINK ABOUT IT

When you read or listen to any advertising, you must approach it critically, using your best judgment to decide if the information is valid or based on fact. In many cases, advertising relies on nonfact or claims, and it contains statements called "faulty generalizations." Faulty generalizations are claims that are made using too few examples. However, they are presented as facts.

Advertising is just one place where you might find evidence of **fact and nonfact.** Other places might be in a newspaper editorial or letter, a report, or any other nonfiction source that claims to be full of facts. Perhaps an author presents a one-sided view: *This article tells me all about how great this car is but offers no statistics on its repair record or its safety record. I can't really trust an article that doesn't give me the whole picture.* Another time, an author might be presenting an opinion as if it were a fact: *The best place in the world to buy seafood is Seattle, Washington.* This statement sounds like a fact, but it is really the author's opinion.

Evaluating Fact and Nonfact

When you are evaluating whether a statement is a fact or nonfact, first decide if what you read can be proved or not. Is there someplace where you could check the fact? Is there missing information? You can take the time to look up the fact, or you can be skeptical based on information that is missing from the text.

Second, use your own best judgment about whether or not a statement is credible, or believable. For example, in the ad for Computease, the author suggests that you can learn everything necessary about computers in three hours. You might evaluate whether this is true based on your own experience: *I have been learning about computers for a long time, and I can think of several times when I have had onscreen tutorials or help when it has taken longer than three hours—and that was just learning about e-mail! So it is hard to believe that any course, no matter how good it is, could teach me everything I ever needed to know in so short a time.*

Third, if necessary, find a reliable resource to check the information you are being given. For an ad, it wouldn't be practical to do this; for other works of nonfiction, it would be useful to check important facts if you feel that statements are not true. Another important point is to decide for yourself what is reliable as a source of information. For example, if you read an article about the rules of baseball and it is written by a seasoned baseball commentator, you would be apt to believe what you read. If you read an article by someone who has only been watching the game for a few seasons, you might not trust the source as much.

Look at the advertisement for Pine Tree Juice Capsules. There are at least four faulty generalizations in the ad. Can you find them? Write them on the lines below. Next to each statement, write why it is a nonfact, or faulty generalization. Compare your answers with a partner.

1. _____

2. _____

3. _____

4. _____

Look at It Another Way

You can use a chart to help you organize your thoughts when you are evaluating facts and nonfacts and their sources. Look at the chart below. In it you will see statements from the Computease Computer Course advertisement. A few examples have been done to show you how to think about evaluating fact and nonfact. Fill in the rest of the chart with information you gather from your prior experience or from outside sources.

Statement	Fact	Nonfact	How I Know
. . . under the advice of expert webmasters . . .		X	
. . . each lesson is fully illustrated with simple line drawings . . .	X		
You simply can't make a mistake, no matter how hard you try!			
You'll learn how to navigate every software system sold on the market today . . . !			

STEP 5: RELATE IT

1. Look at an ad in a slick magazine that doesn't have very many words, but is mostly pictures. What is the ad's main message? What information is the ad suggesting "between the lines"? Cut out the ad and put it in the center of a sheet of poster board. Then draw a web with circles around the picture indicating the various messages the picture is showing. Share your poster with the class. (Visual)

2. Listen to or watch three advertisements on television. They can be local or national ads. Make a list of some faulty generalizations that you hear being made in the ads. Bring your list to class and share them as a basis for further discussion. (Speaking/Listening)

3. Many businesses have advertising or marketing departments of their own who make up advertising slogans. Other companies, particularly large ones, hire advertising agencies to do that work for them. Look up ad agencies (search keywords ad agency, advertising) on the web and peruse them to find out what kind of advertising they do to try to lure customers to use their services. (Technology)

4. Write your own ad for a product that you really believe in. Try to make it as credible as possible so people will be likely to buy it. Remember to use testimonials (statements from people who have used the product) to help back up your credibility. Be sure **not** to use faulty generalizations or nonfacts. (Writing)

ANSWER KEY

Lesson 1: Biography

Test-Taking Strategy, p. 10

1. F	4. F	7. T
2. T	5. T	8. T
3. T	6. F	

Think About It, pp. 11–12

1. SD	4. MI	7. SD
2. SD	5. SD	8. SD
3. SD	6. SD	

Lesson 2: Interview

Check Your Understanding, p. 23
1. b. Austria
2. d. five years
3. b. business
4. a. It singles you out as the best.

Test-Taking Strategy, pp. 24–25
Possible answers:
1. Arnold says that he believes in "staying hungry" which may mean that he believes that if you get "full," you are satisfied, and if you are satisfied, you are no longer reaching for a new goal.
2. This statement though ambiguous, probably means that Arnold feels so at home and happy living in America that, if he believed in reincarnation, he would say he lived in the United States in an earlier life.
3. Arnold probably thinks of a "normal" life as a life in which he wouldn't be striving to win so big. He would be like most people, the "hundreds of thousands" who failed at their dream. (See **Think About It** for model answer.)
4. Answers will vary here. You may need to explain to students that Western philosophy is often thought of as a more materialistic or capitalistic culture than that of the East, which concentrates more on non-material life.

Lesson 3: On-line Research Article

Test-Taking Strategy, pp. 38–39

1. b	3. d	5. b
2. c	4. c	6. d

Lesson 4: Newspaper Columns

Check Your Understanding, pp. 56–57
1. Craig and Patty ventured further than their borders because they were tired of the same old candy and not getting more candy. They wanted more!
2. Craig felt that Halloween was for the treat part of trick-or-treating. His brother was more interested in the "trick" part. First, Craig says that his brother is "too cool to trick-or-treat." Then he goes on to explain all of the tricks he pulled.
3. Craig's brother (and probably some friends) probably followed Craig and Patty on their walk to the houses farther away. (The houses wouldn't have seemed so far away to a 12-year-old.) Then they jumped out of the tree (or perhaps out from behind the tree) and scared them. Evidence is that his brother is "still" laughing, which implies that he was the one who was there to enjoy watching his brother and friend get so scared.
4. Craig probably looked up to his brother ("They were far too cool to trick-or-treat.") He may have also felt some rivalry with his brother (to make matters better. . .). Probably, Craig was pretty mad at his brother for playing a trick on him.
5. Goodman kept watching the man "caress" the bicycle and felt inspired to say something to make the man feel good about his bike.
6. Goodman may have felt disappointed by her presents, but knew better than to disappoint her parents by telling them so.

7. Possible answer: We look back at what we really wanted for a present and decide that our children must want the same thing we do. This statement has a deeper meaning, though. It suggests that we give people what we want rather than what they want, assuming that everyone wants the same thing we do.

8. Careful people listen to each other. Goodman means that if you really listen to someone else's needs and wants, maybe you can choose the right gift. Beyond the very specific idea of a gift, she means that if you really listen to someone, then you can know what they like and don't like and really hear them and acknowledge what they want.

Think About It, pp. 59–60
How the articles are alike: (Possible answers)
1. They are both written by newspaper columnists.
2. They are both written in the first person.
3. They are both stories about things that happened to the author.
4. They both use details to bring the story to life.
5. They both use informal writing style.
6. They are both describing events that happen around holidays.

How the articles are different: (Possible answers)
1. The Wilson column is funny, where the Goodman column is provocative.
2. The Wilson column tells about an event long ago, the Goodman column tells about a fairly recent event.
3. Wilson's column is a personal story, where Goodman's article begins as a personal story but then becomes a more objective observation.

Lesson 5: Speech

Check Your Understanding, pp. 71–72
1. Dr. King was hoping that his listeners would be inspired to act—he tells them to go back to their cities and spread the word that things have changed.

2. Repeating Phrases:
   One hundred years later . . .
   Now is the time . . .
   We cannot be satisfied . . .
   Go back to . . .
   I have a dream . . .
   Let freedom ring . . .
3. Imagery:
   "The Negro lives on *a lonely island* . . ."
   " . . . crippled by the manacles . . ."
   " . . . to lift our nation from the quicksands of racial injustice to the solid rock . . ."
   "justice rolls down like waters . . ."
   " . . . oasis of freedom and justice."
4. Quotes:
   "Unalienable rights of life, liberty, and the pursuit of happiness." (Declaration of Independence)
   " . . . glory of the Lord shall be revealed . . . all flesh . . ." (Bible)
   "My country 'tis of thee . . ." ("My Country 'Tis of Thee"—song)
   "Free at last! Free at last! Thank God Almighty, we are free at last!" (African-American spiritual song)

Test-Taking Strategy, pp. 72–73
1. a
2. c

Think About It, pp. 73–74
Simile:
" . . . until justice rolls down *like* waters and righteousness *like* a mighty stream . . ."

Lesson 6: Advertisements

Check Your Understanding, p. 84
1. c. three hours
2. c. computer beginners
3. d. They lubricate your system.
4. c. decrease your appetite

Think About It, pp. 87–88
Here are five faulty generalizations:
1. The capsules are "now available . . . with incredible life-changing results!" (Who says that they are life-changing? In what way are they life-changing?)

2. These capsules "work better than anything you've ever tried." (How do they know? On what statistic are they basing this statement?)

3. "This makes it possible to virtually eliminate fat deposits all over your body." (The key word here is *"virtually." Virtual* means "almost entirely." This "almost" leaves plenty of room for exceptions, so the makers of the capsules don't have to stand behind this claim.

4. The ingredients contained in "[t]he pine needle juice capsules transmit orders to the fat cells. . . ." (You can call on your common sense and prior knowledge here. You know that no capsule can "transmit orders" to any cells. The authors here have assigned human powers to a pill!)

Share Your Bright Ideas with Us!

We want to hear from you! Your valuable comments and suggestions will help us meet your current and future classroom needs.

Your name_____Date_____

School name_____Phone_____

School address_____

Grade level taught_____Subject area(s) taught_____Average class size_____

Where did you purchase this publication?_____

Was your salesperson knowledgeable about this product?   Yes_____   No_____

What monies were used to purchase this product?

____School supplemental budget   ____Federal/state funding   ____Personal

Please "grade" this Walch publication according to the following criteria:

	A	B	C	D	F
Quality of service you received when purchasing	A	B	C	D	F
Ease of use	A	B	C	D	F
Quality of content	A	B	C	D	F
Page layout	A	B	C	D	F
Organization of material	A	B	C	D	F
Suitability for grade level	A	B	C	D	F
Instructional value	A	B	C	D	F

COMMENTS:_____

_____

What specific supplemental materials would help you meet your current—or future—instructional needs?

_____

Have you used other Walch publications? If so, which ones?_____

May we use your comments in upcoming communications?   ____Yes   ____No

Please **FAX** this completed form to **207-772-3105**, or mail it to:

Product Development, J. Weston Walch, Publisher, P.O. Box 658, Portland, ME 04104-0658

We will send you a **FREE GIFT** as our way of thanking you for your feedback. **THANK YOU!**